RED COAT DIARIES

RED COAT DIARIES

True Stories from the
Royal Canadian Mounted Police

Edited by Constable Aaron Sheedy

mosaic press

Library and Archives Canada Cataloguing in Publication

Red coat diaries : true stories from the Royal Canadian Mounted Police / edited by Aaron Sheedy.

ISBN 978-0-88962-935-6

1. Royal Canadian Mounted Police--Anecdotes.
I. Sheedy, Aaron, 1973-

HV8158.7.R69R43 2011   363.20971   C2011-905971-1

Published by Mosaic Press, offices and warehouse at 1252 Speers Road, Units 1 and 2, Oakville, Ontario, L6L 5N9, Canada and Mosaic Press, 40 Sonwil Dr, Cheektowaga, NY14225, U.S.A.

Copyright © The authors, 2011

2nd printing, 2012

ISBN 978-0-88962-935-6

Ebook 978-0-88962-944-8

Designed by Keith Daniel

We acknowledge the financial support of the Government of Canada through the Canada Book Fund (CBF) for this project.

Nous reconnaissons l'aide finan-cière du gouvernement du Canada par l'entremise du Fonds du livre du Canada (FLC) pour ce projet.

Canadian Heritage   Patrimoine canadien

Canada

Mosaic Press in Canada:
1252 Speers Road, Units 1 & 2
Oakville, Ontario
L6L 5N9
Phone/Fax: 905-825-2130
info@mosaic-press.com

Mosaic Press in U.S.A.:
c/o Livingston, 40 Sonwil Dr,
Cheektowaga, NY
14225
Phone/Fax: 905-825-2130
info@mosaic-press.com

www.mosaic-press.com

In Memory of

Constable Christopher Worden

Constable Douglas Scott

Sergeant John Storer

We continue to tell your stories.

TABLE OF CONTENTS

Part III: A Time for Action

My experience with the Royal Canadian Mounted Police (RCMP) is unique, as are the experiences of the contributors to this book. Fortunately, my story is not one that is shared by many.

My journey in the RCMP did not begin at Depot. I do not arrest criminals on a daily basis. I do not put myself in harm's way, day in and day out, to protect the lives of Canadians. I am a federal public servant, working as a leadership consultant in the RCMP's Learning and Development section in Ottawa, Ontario. When I began this job in January 2009, it was not my first exposure to the RCMP. My life within the RCMP family began when I married Constable Chris Worden in 2003.

I lived the life of an RCMP spouse in the Northwest Territories for nearly five years. I adapted to the life of my husband, who worked shifts and was often "on call". My vocabulary grew to include a multitude of acronyms, as I tried to keep up with all of the "blue-world" talk in which I became immersed. I even earned a paycheque guarding cells occasionally in the isolated, two-person detachment in the northern settlement of Wha Ti, Northwest Territories, where we lived for nearly two years. I learned how to operate a two-way radio, use ten codes, drive snow machines and boats, and was able to prompt my husband with the standard questions when calls from the telecoms operator came into the house in the middle of the night. This was my life as a Mountie's wife up North, and I loved it.

This all changed on October 6, 2007 when I received the worst news that an RCMP family member could receive. Chris had been killed while on duty in Hay River. My life as I had known it ended. I had now joined the unofficial club of RCMP widows.

It may sound cliché, but the RCMP is a huge family. They took me in when I married a member (RCMP officers are known as "members"), and they were there to support me through the planning of a regimental funeral and the preparation and signing of documents. They kept me informed (as much as they could) of the investigation and legal proceedings, assisted me when I decided to move out of the North, and continually offered to provide support in any way they could to our family.

In the months after the two shootings in the North that claimed the lives of both Chris and Constable Douglas Scott, I became very vocal in the media about the lack of a backup policy and the need for the RCMP to keep their membership safer. I wanted the Force to move quickly on changing officer safety procedures. I have been asked, on many occasions, "How can you work for the RCMP after what happened to you?" My answer is relatively simple: I want to be part of the solution. I want to make things better.

The RCMP is highlighted daily by the media with stories it believes will capture the interests of the greatest audience. Unfortunately, these stories focus on the occurrences that illustrate a dramatic event or the perceived questionable behaviour of a small percentage of RCMP employees. Sweeping generalizations are then made about the quality and leadership of the RCMP. This type of reporting frustrates me because there are so many instances, every day, that involve RCMP employees providing a positive service to their communities, but these do not reach the eyes or ears of the general public.

The people in the RCMP work every day to protect those who have chosen to live in Canada. Sure, as in any large organization, there are opportunities to improve on existing policies and procedures, and there are employees who make poor decisions on occasion. It is unfortunate, however, that these issues make front page news ahead of the stories where Mounties have made a sexual assault victim safe and comfortable enough to tell his or her story, so that charges can be laid and the perpetrator stopped from victimizing someone else. Or instead of when a member goes into a local school to teach young students about the debilitating influence and effects of drugs and alcohol through the D.A.R.E. Program. Or ahead of the team of operators who remove a drug dealer from the streets so that a life is not unnecessarily taken, and somebody else won't have to receive the news that I did.

Working for the RCMP allows me to give back to the people who protect our country. Helping to design and create leadership programs within the Force gives me the opportunity to enhance employees' careers, while simultaneously contributing to a better prepared and competent organization. It gives me a purpose—a purpose that I am proud of.

I was honoured and humbled when approached about writing this foreword. I feel that the stories shared in this book illustrate the dedication and human perspective of each author. It is the human perspective of the RCMP organization that I experienced and continue to advocate for. These are the stories that need to be shared to promote the continued positive efforts of our employees. It is my belief that if more people are exposed to this side of its employees, and the RCMP organization as a whole, public perception will change. There is power in education. I am grateful for the efforts of Aaron Sheedy and to the RCMP for allowing these stories to be shared, and, thus, enabling the public to get a glimpse of the positive aspects of the RCMP.

I salute all the men and women who have contributed to this book and all those who continually risk their lives to assist others. You have the support of those who understand your world. You are doing your part to educate others who have limited exposure to the life led by an RCMP officer. I applaud you for your contributions to the individuals and communities you serve. You will forever have my full support.

Jodie Worden
Ottawa, Ontario

ACKNOWLEDGMENTS

A couple years ago, I was having coffee with a friend who knows the RCMP well. As we talked he asked me, "Why can't the RCMP show Canadians who they really are?" He went on to explain that he has always found us to be a group of alert and intelligent people, filled with humour and compassion. But that message, those stories, somehow, in his experience, never get told. Those comments prompted the idea for this book, and I reached out to Mosaic Press to help make it a reality. As the project progressed so did my list of people who deserved recognition for their contributions.

First and foremost, I thank the contributors. As well as providing the content, their willingness to volunteer their time and share their experiences is a tribute to the spirit that I hope this book captures.

My best friend and the love of my life, my wife, Yolanda Romanec, played several roles in this project including website developer, desktop publisher, photographer, and content/copy editor. Yolanda, thank you for making us look so good!

Edgar Cowan, Howard Aster, Keith Daniel and the gang at Mosaic Press, have my thanks for their guidance and patience, but also for their unflinching commitment to Canadian literature and to new writers.

Within the RCMP and the RCMP Foundation, sincere thanks to Sheila Bird, Superintendent Tim Cogan, Superintendent Greg Peters, Inspector Carole Bird, Sergeant Pat Flood, Fred Semerjian, Chris Power, and all the people who helped with the digital media both at the national and divisional levels. And finally, everyone who lifted a telephone, or sent an email, or had a meeting in support of this project.

I would like to thank my policing role models and friends at the Toronto Airport Detachment, the members of the "O" Division Tactical Troop, and my fellow drug-dog handlers and trainers for all the adventures over the years.

Thanks also to my close friends Paul Shaughnessy and Kathy Horton for their friendship, support, and expert literary insights.

Special thanks to my brothers and sister, and the rest of my family and friends for their ongoing love. Last but certainly not least, I thank my mother, Clara Lovatt, for passing on the creative gene and my father, Glen Sheedy, for buying me a typewriter. That typewriter really changed everything.

I truly believe that the collective work here is greater than the sum of its parts, and it has been my honour to work with the contributors over the past two years to bring our stories to you.

I would like to know what you think. You can send me your thoughts and comments through my website, **www.oldschoolproductions.ca.**

Maintiens le droit.

Constable Aaron Sheedy
Toronto, Ontario

PART I

Adventures in Far-Off Places

THE HOME TEAM
Constable April Dequanne
Toronto, Ontario

As I travelled from Toronto, Ontario to Whale Cove, Nunavut, I was progressively awakened to the reality of what I had gotten myself into. It was just a month posting, to give relief to a Mountie in Whale Cove who was going on vacation. But as the series of connections landed and took off between Toronto and Whale Cove, the passengers transformed from business, to casual, to what looked like the cast of *Never Cry Wolf*. Massive goose down coats, huge boots, and real fur hoods were the norm. The plane I was on was travelling in front of a winter storm, and for the leg into Rankin Inlet the pilot told us that he was going to, "Chance it." (Excuse me?)

Safely on the ground, I zipped up my fancy Gortex jacket and popped a toque on my head. With confidence in my high-tech gear, I exited the plane for the fifty-yard dash across the tarmac to the airport. In that short time, the wind managed to freeze the moist air around my mouth and nose, even the tiny hairs on my face. It froze my tearing eyes shut and blew right through my jacket. A man walked by and whispered, "Fight nature with nature." I turned to see the man who spoke this wisdom but he didn't stop. He was dressed in a seal skin jacket with a hood trimmed in fox fur, a pair of tall moccasins (*kamiks*), and polar bear fur mitts.

With the cultural and environmental shock behind me, I settled into my work and the enjoyment of exploring and discovering the people and environment of Whale Cove. The people were very welcoming and I had several local experiences I will remember my entire life. I was invited out on snowmobile trips, I witnessed the pride and generosity of two hunters who brought their kill (three muskox) back to share with their neighbours. I was humbled to witness, that in a community where food was incredibly expensive, the instinct to share was still so strong. I also got to see the kids enjoy the stuffed animals that were donated by the people who work in my home detachment. For many of those kids, the donated stuffed animals were the only toys they had.

One afternoon, Tom, the gym teacher from Inuglak School, called and asked if I would be interested in taking his place in a hockey game that night. After hibernating for three weeks, I welcomed the exercise. Tom's equipment was a good fit except for gloves, helmet, and skates. I began to ask some of the kids who were hanging around the arena for the required items. Surprised, many of them asked, "You gonna play hockey?" and offered up their gear. Eight-year-old Paul Qiok had just the right size skates and helmet for me. I put on the gear and laced up the skates in the foyer of the arena, as there was no change room available to me.

The young boys and girls gathered around and filled the remaining time with questions: *You gonna play with the guys? You ever play hockey before? Why are you playing hockey? Are you afraid? Can you skate?* They had never seen a girl play hockey before.

The "Home" team looked young and strong. They were a group of guys who had grown up together surviving the harsh climate and playing one of the few sports available to them. We, the "Visiting" team, with the help of some locals, were not so young and strong, and not as acclimatized to the harsh climate and way of life. I stepped on the ice and skated to blend in with everyone during the warm-up.

The ice's surface was cold and fast. No artificial ice there, it was the real thing. The players sharpened their skates by hand and got their hockey equipment during trips out. With the bare essentials, these kids grew up playing Canada's sport the way it started, and with skills that would shame even some of the best hockey players I know. I figured that many were just waiting to be discovered. Jordin Tootoo, from nearby Rankin Inlet, was and now he plays in the NHL. When I stepped on the ice I thought I was playing against the Nashville Predators. Many were wearing hand-me-down jerseys and NHL replica jerseys with Tootoo (#22) on their backs. It was evident that Tootoo was a local hero.

It wasn't long before word spread and the arena started to fill with spectators. They were there to see if a girl could actually play hockey. The puck dropped, and in the faceoff circle I saw him—a bootlegger from the community who was the bane of my existence and the subject of many calls to duty while I was in Whale Cove. He was on the young and strong team.

"I'm going to get creamed," I thought as we made brief eye contact.

I kept my head up and stayed clear of the corners—I'd never stepped on the ice with a guy I had arrested before. He was young, strong, and quick and knew how to handle the puck. Just days earlier, when I arrested him, I had the upper hand with my training and "tools" of the job. Now, I felt uncomfortably vulnerable as the playing field was heavily tilted in his favour. I had stepped onto his ice.

The game was quick paced and the opposition had no idea a girl was playing. That made me feel like I was holding my own out there. I even took a couple of hits, picked myself up, and kept skating. The score was six to four for the Home team. We seized the chance for a breakaway during a bad line change by the Home team. From my left wing, I dipped quickly to the middle near centre ice, and found the puck on my stick. I skated with all I had toward the net; this was my chance to contribute to the score. I could hear the cold ice being split behind me by the blades of what I hoped was a teammate. He skated past me, tapped my stick, and tried to grab the puck. I fought hard to keep the puck, dipped left, and fired the shot from the top of the faceoff circle just before I took the hit. The puck hit the goalie's stick, popped up between his pads, and trickled into the net. The crowd cheered and "oohed". From my crumpled position on the ice I celebrated the goal, and grabbed the hand that offered to pick me up. It was him, my work-life nemesis. "Lucky shot," he said and skated away. We were losing but it was okay because the crowd was cheering. They were chanting my name! Girls, women, boys, and men alike were chanting my name every time I stepped on the ice. I felt like Jordin Tootoo, a local hero.

After the game, in the comfort of my apartment, I iced a bruise that I decided I would not tell anyone about. A knock on the door made me jump, as my apartment was connected to the detachment and it could have been an emergency. I opened the door and it was him. "You did really great out there, and I just want you to have this." He handed me a sweaty jersey bearing an inukshuk on the front, covered in cologne to mask the smell. "We play again next Thursday, if you want."

When my posting was over I arrived back in Toronto on a Wednesday, late in the evening. I exited the plane in boots and heavy winter jacket. I realized that many people on my connecting flight from Ottawa looked at me inquisitively. I had refused to remove my layers of clothing. I had earned bragging rights, and I wanted people to know that I had just returned from a part of Canada's most beautiful North. Assunai Whale Cove!

AFGHANISTAN
Constable Jeffery Hirsch
Halifax, Nova Scotia

Baking in a thirty degree afternoon sun, Sergeant Ali Hussein and I weave our way through wide, dirt alleys in the Loya Wala neighbourhood of Kandahar City. Sergeant Hussein is a rare commodity among Afghan policemen. He is literate, educated, and patient. He wears his hair short, face shaven, and uniform neat. I encourage him to knock on some compound doors and talk to the local people. Sergeant Hussein walks up to a metal door embedded into a dried mud wall that stands eight-feet-tall. He raps firmly and the blue door shakes loosely in the wood frame. After a minute, a tall man with black ruffled hair opens the door and smiles at Sergeant Hussein. He is covered in fresh mud and his hands are caked with the wet sludge. The man explains he is repairing his interior walls and he excuses himself for not shaking hands. He tells us that he has recently moved to Kandahar City and doesn't know his neighbours yet.

Unlike most other neighbourhoods, Loya Wala does not have a reputation for close family and tribal ties. Loya Wala was city-owned land which, since the Taliban lost power, has been claimed and squatted on by returning displaced Afghans from all over the country. There are more improvised explosive devices (IEDs) targeting the police in this one district each month than the rest of the city altogether.

I am leaned in tight to my interpreter, a young Pashto man in his twenties, nicknamed "Elvis". I rely on him to translate what is being said, but I am also trying to watch the body language between Sergeant Hussein and the man he is speaking with.

"It's very important," I explained to Sergeant Hussein and his policemen before the patrol, "that we listen to the people and see how they react to us being in their neighbourhood."

This quiet, triangular-shaped neighbourhood, only five minutes from the police station, was recently the scene of an IED strike on Afghan policemen. Fortunately none of them died, but two of the men were still in the hospital a week later with concussions and blown ear drums. The neighbourhood is made up of low, one story, mud-wall compounds that house multiple families and often a few sheep. There is no electricity and no plumbing. Open sewers run every few metres and garbage piles are scattered on every corner, waiting for pickup that rarely comes. There is only one communal water pump (a hand pump) where most of the children are gathered today, watching us and giggling as we methodically move along.

Something has changed here in recent weeks and we needed to show a presence to reassure the Kandaharis that live here and support the police, that they won't be abandoned just because the police were attacked in this area. Likewise, we need to show whoever planted the device that we won't be scared off. This is easily my twentieth patrol in the ninth district of Kandahar City. Many Canadian soldiers know this district as well as I do, but to me I feel intimately responsible for it and accountable for what happens here. If the police fail to secure this district, it may be seen as a failure of our training and mentoring efforts. I am an RCMP officer whose main role over a twelve-month period is to train and mentor the Afghan Uniform Police (AUP) of District Nine, along with two other districts totalling one hundred and fifty AUP of all ranks and abilities.

Surrounding Sergeant Hussein and me is a section of Canadian infantry from our base, Camp Nathan Smith. The soldiers are an even mix of regular army from the Royal Canadian Regiment in New Brunswick (2RCR) and reservists from across Canada. Even with this experienced force protection element, I am still on alert. You are always in a "red zone" when you are on patrol because every member is part of a team responsible for each other's safety. Most important, I am a crucial link, through my translator, to help the AUP react properly during the patrol, especially if we are ambushed or encounter an explosive device.

There are six other AUP with us, all of whom I have gotten to know this summer while mentoring them during their meagre eight weeks of basic training. The AUP form the head and tail of our foot patrol as we snake through the neighbourhood. This way, they are the first and last security presence the people will see and, hopefully, eventually trust. They are alert, though they seem less talkative with the locals than Sergeant Hussein. I am hoping that they will see his behaviour and copy him, so I ensure that I heap a large amount of praise upon Sergeant Hussein in front of his men when we get back to the police station. Our foot patrol lasts just an hour and, with the heat and empty water bottles in the policemen's hands, I know that it has been enough.

For me, the patrol has been only three hours from beginning to end. We mounted up in our armoured vehicles and convoyed to the police station, planned the patrol with Sergeant Hussein on his new map table, courtesy of the Government of Canada, and conducted some brief rehearsals with his men before starting the patrol. I organized the mission today to assess Sergeant Hussein's planning skills and leadership, and he executed a textbook patrol. With the post-patrol review complete, I will head back to the relative security of our base where I will shower off the sweat and dirt, eat until I'm full, call home, and perhaps watch a movie.

Sergeant Hussein will still be at his police station while I turn the fan on to cool my room. Sergeant Hussein will likely have only a little bread and some lamb and rice for supper. Perhaps he'll have some clean warm water to drink and clean with, if his headquarters found enough gas to run the water truck to the station today. With no electricity, and little gas to run a generator, he will likely write up his daily report using a small, propane-powered light. He will have to hope that the men he assigns to guard the towers of the police station don't fall asleep, as they so often do. Worse, he will have to watch that they don't use drugs or desert their post altogether. As difficult as it was for me to spend a year away from family and friends back in Canada, I feel deeply for Sergeant Hussein who will face this hardship, living in the "red zone" daily, likely for the rest of his life.

The history of Afghanistan is so complicated and so troubled; I don't think anyone can summarize it in anything less than a thousand page thesis, so I won't try here. I believe it's enough to say that Afghanistan is a country of extremes. There is extreme poverty, extreme corruption, and extreme hardship. The land transitions from sandy deserts, to rocky barrens, to lush green valleys, to impassable mountains. It's a country made up of a million shades of brown, dotted by small valleys of emerald green where mulberry and pomegranate orchards thrive. Travelling across Kandahar Province, you will see irrigated grape and melon fields that crisscross the spaces between hills and mountains. Then there are, of course, the forests of marihuana plants and fields of poisonous poppy plants that are deceptively beautiful shades of purple, white, and pink when in bloom. Rivers that glow a brilliant turquoise colour can be seen alongside roads and villages. The rivers are beyond polluted, as untreated sewage flows into them and people wash their cars, laundry, cattle, and themselves along the river banks.

Summer temperatures regularly push the thermometer needle off the scale, past forty degrees Celsius. We comfort ourselves by saying at least it's only a dry heat. With so little moisture, the daily weather report is always brilliant, clear blue skies with no cloud cover. I have seen only two bursts of rain in four months. Late summer brings with it afternoon sand storms that turn the sky the colour of cinnamon, and send everyone running to close windows and doors. Winter is dry and rarely dips below minus ten. The people of Kandahar, who have mostly denuded their land of firewood and can't afford coal, send their children out daily to collect garbage to burn in stoves for warmth. Yes, childhood is extreme in Afghanistan as well. The lucky few in urban centres are increasingly attending schools. Many children as young as eight or nine are often seen helping their fathers tend a flock of sheep or hauling drinking water for the family in plastic jugs, all the while carrying around their younger siblings.

The RCMP first landed on the ground in Kandahar in 2005 with a small team whose job was to assess the capabilities of the AUP, and what potential existed for Canadian police to mentor and increase the ability of the Afghan police to provide true policing services in the fledgling democracy. The Canadian commitment to train, mentor, and advise the Afghan police now exceeds forty deployed Canadian police personnel (administered by the RCMP International Peace Operations branch) from across Canada. I had the pleasure of working with officers from Sudbury, Montreal, Ottawa, Durham, and numerous other RCMP detachments. We all came from different policing backgrounds. Some of us were tactical instructors, forensic technicians, explosive-techs, and experienced supervisors. We all brought a different specialized knowledge to the table and many, like me, had Canadian military service in our background which helped us integrate with our Canadian Forces colleagues. In 2007, the United States put up funds and US Army Police Mentor Teams to push forward a new concept called Focused District Development (FDD).

As part of FDD, Afghanistan's provinces each had a different country responsible for it. Canada took on Kandahar and set-up the Kandahar Provincial Reconstruction Team. The team was based at Camp Nathan Smith, an abandoned fruit canning factory smack in the middle of Kandahar City.

Every single Afghan police officer in the district, from commander to new recruit, was sent to the Regional Training Centre outside Kandahar City for eight weeks. They were drug tested, interviewed, and truly unsuitable candidates were let go. During the basic training, we went with them and, alongside contracted US trainers, we taught basic skills such as weapons handling and searching people. We reviewed human rights and community policing concepts as well, but this was challenging and often didn't sink in for the illiterate policemen who had never sat in a classroom in their lives. We were also dealing with interpreters of questionable ability. When the police graduated eight weeks later, they were given new uniforms, new equipment, and reinserted back into their districts. Of note, the drug use by the AUP who completed basic training almost vanished when they returned to their districts, a testimony to the success of the zero-tolerance philosophy of drug use during the training.

The training program didn't address everything though, and many of us in CIVPOL (the Civilian Police Contingent) found extra training and projects that needed to be done to fill in huge gaps in police capabilities. Some members focussed on weapons, body guarding, IED, or forensic identification training. For me, the eighty to ninety percent illiteracy rate among Afghan policemen was a glaring weakness that was undermining all our efforts. The existing language training system was corrupt, siphoning money to Afghan government officials who didn't have the ability to teach, and often falsified records in order to pad their Canadian paycheque. I quickly cancelled the program while trying to think of another way forward.

In mid-July, I headed out on a foot patrol through Kandahar City to assess the police of District Five. We stepped out the main gate of our camp and began what was planned to be a two hour patrol in the community around our camp. At the height of summer, each hour we would easily drink a litre of water that we carried in a bladder on our backs without the urge to urinate. We were each carrying twenty pounds of equipment in addition to our helmets, twenty-five pounds of body armour, a rifle, and a pistol. Every few hundred metres we sought out some piece of shade and an opportunity to squat and talk with the locals.

As we continued the patrol, we came across a large family whose compound doors were wide open. We peered in and saw the family hard at work tending a garden of massive rose bushes coloured bright peach and red standing on five-foot-high canes. The family was intensely proud and introduced their sixteen-year-old son to us who had studied journalism in

Kabul the last year. His English was passable and we made small talk before moving on. Random encounters with Afghans who are struggling against the odds to make a better life for themselves always renewed my faith that Afghanistan may not be cursed forever.

Surrounded once again by the Canadian soldiers in a protective bubble around me, I spoke with Afghan Police Sergeant Bashir about the police under his command. He told me that he had just over half of his allotted officers for his district. The usual stories of equipment shortages, lack of pay, fuel, and food were told. But when I asked him how many of his men could read and write, he lit up! He told me that he convinced five of his men to pay a few dollars a month and they hired a teacher to come to the police station a few times a week to teach them. Afghan solutions for Afghan problems are truly the best ones and I embraced Sergeant Bashir's idea.

Over the next six months after that patrol, I submitted numerous proposals and held meetings that culminated in February 2009 with the start of a new AUP literacy project. I obtained Canadian support to hire seventeen teachers from the Kandahar Ministry of Education to travel to police stations up to four times a week for a year and deliver the adult literacy course to the policemen right at their police station. The goal was three hundred functionally literate policemen. The total cost for the teachers' salaries and equipment to run the program for a year was less than that of a single police officer's salary in Canada.

Canada was also committed to building new police stations for the Afghans. For example, we worked closely with Canadian Forces engineers to design a new secure police station for the Dand District south of Kandahar City. To ensure we had community support, I headed out on a patrol to review the blueprints with the district *shura*, which is essentially a town council of respected elders. The new design would include construction of walls and towers that would surround the police station and the two-story school it protects.

During the patrol, I met with District Leader Amadullah Nazik and the District Police Commander Shamsulhaq. Colonel Shamsulhaq used to be in the Afghan National Army, but after his two brothers were killed fighting the Taliban he accepted the responsibility of taking on his brother's wives and eight children to raise as his own. He transferred to the AUP for more stability, but continues to be increasingly frustrated with the corruption he encounters every day. Shamsulhaq has a huge smile and is highly regarded by his men as an intelligent leader. We drank hot chai tea that was served in dirty glass cups, as we sat cross-legged on cushions in his office. It gave me a chance to take off my helmet and drop the gear I was carrying beside me. My rifle leaned up in the corner and, with my Canadian soldier protection close by, I had the chance to focus on forming a friendship with Shamsulhaq over stories and a snack of raisins and almonds. These bonds, forged not only through joint patrolling and training, but through sharing a meal and small talk, are crucial for developing trust and confidence in one another.

I found I had to overcome the obstacles of language difficulties and cultural differences so I could embrace the experience, master the use of my interpreter, and make an emotional investment in my role as mentor. It's important to learn some local language, though it's not realistic to expect fluency. The local languages of Pashto or the more Persian Dari, are famously difficult with different dialects from one village to the next. I learned basic greetings and battlefield commands, should I need them. I could always bring a smile to an Afghan policeman's face by clapping him on the back and saying, "Darisha," which means "very good" when they have completed a task well.

I experienced some things in life that are so vibrant, so unique, and so meaningful, that no nuance or subtle detail is ever lost when I recount it. Any single day in Afghanistan provided a rich, larger than life experience. The constant smell of burning garbage, the droning call to Morning Prayer over the mosque loud speaker, the roar of an armoured vehicle's diesel engine, and the incredible smiles on the faces of brightly dressed children will always stay with me.

Opening a newly built police station, and the scene of Afghan policemen setting-up their chairs and desks and waiting for their literacy teacher to arrive are also unforgettably rewarding images. I was extremely pleased to hear, a couple years after my tour was over, that the literacy program not only continued but actually thrived and is a source of pride for the AUP.

Afghanistan is now a shared experience for many Canadians. Thousands of Canadian men and women have served there and brought their families along for the ride through emails, photographs, and the rare phone call home. What many Canadians don't realize is that there are a growing number of police officers that have walked alongside our soldiers in that tortured land. We have lost friends and colleagues while serving Canada, and we've called Afghanistan home for up to a year of our lives. It was a privilege to work and live alongside so many incredible Canadian police officers and soldiers and do our small part towards bringing security and peace to Afghanistan.

ONE IN A HUNDRED
Constable Tony Deuters (Ret.)
Gastonia, North Carolina

It was 1952. I was twenty-two-years-old, and I was standing in the RCMP recruiting office in Montreal, and I had just signed on the dotted line. I was a Mountie, I was beside myself. I swore allegiance to the Crown, and we were told that we were one in a hundred and the best of many. My drill instructor at Depot would have a much different opinion of me and my cohorts, but I couldn't have known that standing proudly in Montreal as I received my travel instructions.

With visions of the Pass Out Ceremony, that would have me and my friends marching in the scarlet red tunics called the "Red Serge" and being fully engaged as Mounties, I boarded the train from Montreal to Regina.

The "Canadian" train that crossed Canada by the Canadian Pacific Railway had shiny, new stainless steel rail cars, with domes so we could see all around us, as we slipped through Quebec, Ontario, and Manitoba. It was a fitting journey, I thought, for a pack of Canada's newest public servants to make their way across the country in such style.

It was 3:00 AM when we rolled into Regina, Saskatchewan. It was a new definition of both dark and cold for me. But we made it! We were here!

One of the first orders of business for our troop of recruits was to meet our drill instructor, Bill Perry. I think that the drill instructors must have stayed up at night inventing the most inhumane names they could call us. I couldn't imagine ever repeating those things. Looking back, the congratulations from the recruiter in Montreal must have been an inside joke, to inflate our egos and then to send us to Depot to face drill.

Horses and equestrian training were a big part of Depot in the 1950s. Traditionally, we, the RCMP, were a cavalry, with the commissioned officers on horseback and everyone else carried supplies, as the horses were too valuable for such labour. In fact, when it came time to bring the cannons into battles, the horses would be kept at a safe distance and the RCMP members would run into the battle hauling the heavy cannons and supplies. Our horsemanship has a long history, spanning back to the founding of Canada and the gold rush in the Yukon. It was from these early times that the famous "Musical Ride" was born. We were made keenly aware of the pedigree of the RCMP equestrian program during our time at Depot. In fact, when we got enough experience, we were given the proud name of a Ride (a troop). We were known as Ride G, and we were immediately rewarded with an ice-cold shower by the senior troop as hazing.

Depot was like that: command and control. The instructors were in charge, with the most feared being the drill instructors. But there was also a hierarchy of troops, where the senior troops were expected to maintain the discipline of the junior troops. I remember thinking that the senior troops were so much more qualified than I was, when in fact they had only a month or sometimes just a couple weeks more experience. Junior troops sat at the back of the Mess Hall. They couldn't wear their boots, they had to wear runners. They couldn't walk on the sidewalks. They couldn't decide what to watch on the TV at Depot.

As the weeks went on we became proficient riders, at least in our own minds, picturing ourselves on the Musical Ride as we trotted and cantered our horses around the ring. Our mounts, however, would just be nonchalantly going around the riding ring, minding their own business, neither challenged nor interested in what we were doing on their backs.

Suspended in the rafters of the riding ring was a large, black ball known as "The Ball of Fear". Somehow, the horses were conditioned to be terrified of this orb. When the riding instructor lowered the Ball of Fear into the centre of the riding ring the horses' ears pinned back and they became ultra-alert, as they prepared to deal with the unholy terror before them. The riding ring was an oval, so the sides were much narrower than the length. As a result, when the horse approached the side of the ring they would be closer to the ball and would race to the longer end. As there was no warning of this behaviour, we were surprised when our horse took off like a shot! The animal then would walk as slowly as it could until it got to the narrow side and then—bang! Off it went as fast as it could to clear the perceived danger of the ball. Many of us would fall ass-over-tea-kettle and end up covered in the mucky, soft dirt of the riding ring. All the horses wanted was to be as far from that ball as they could, and, as God made little apples, nothing was going to stop them, certainly not the riding novices playing make-believe Musical Ride on their backs.

That experience was a great equalizer: farm boys who were usually the horse-masters were laying in the muck with the street-wise city kids. So many lessons were learned on the floor of the riding ring.

Our troop partook in another equestrian adventure that ended in a similar fashion to our Ball of Fear experience. One weekend we decided that we were going to have a picnic. We took a collection for groceries, invited a compliment of local girls, and got permission from a farmer north of the city to use his field for the picnic. Not being allowed to marry until we'd been in the Force for five years, and living in troop formation (no privacy) at Depot really cramped any chance we had with the girls. Encouraged by beer, Canadian Club whisky, and testosterone, we had an overwhelming desire to show off our horsemanship for the girls. But the only four-legged animals around were...cows.

Once again, we were reminded of how our ability compared to our training with the RCMP horses. The cows seemed so docile standing in that field, but when descended upon by a group of drunk want-to-be Mounties, cows can be quite quick and, when cornered, downright dangerous. For a second time, we were handed our humility by a quadruped, this time in front of a collection of civilian girls!

The girls weren't impressed. As it turned out, neither was the farmer, so he called the Regina City Police. As the Regina boys arrived, we figured that we'd be able to talk down some fellow cops, but they weren't impressed either. Escorting recruits back to Depot was a common duty for the Regina City Police, and their reward for the escort was informing our drill instructor. And he rounded out the list of people who were not impressed with us. Although he never said so, I believe he saw the humour in our adventure. Nonetheless, we pulled extra stable duty, a fitting punishment for being escorted back to base by the local police.

Finally it was our turn to be senior troop. The end was in sight. Our minds were turning to our future posts and to leaving Depot and going out to the real world again.

One of the responsibilities of senior troop was, "Stable Parade". On Sunday morning the troop had to muck out the stables, fill the troughs, and re-stack the manger with straw and oats. There is clean and then there is RCMP *clean*. You could eat off the floor after we had cross swept and hosed out every fiber of debris from the stables. Those horses lived well.

As we were walking back to the barracks from Stable Parade, the other troops attacked us! With a five to one majority, we had no defense. We were all introduced to the shame of being dunked in the water trough one by one. At Depot, attacking a senior troop was the equivalent of a coup d'état and the gauntlet had been dropped. We learned that the whole affair was planned and led by another senior troop. No senior troop should ever rise against a fellow senior troop no matter what the reason. This could not be ignored.

The revenge plan was to attack them before sunrise and ransack their barracks, tear apart their beds, overturn their mattresses, and basically just give them a good ragging so they would have to spend the morning putting their barracks back together before inspection.

Just before morning light, we slipped out into the dark and around the back of our building, through the alley by the blacksmith shop, and surrounded H Troop's barracks. There were two doors, one at the rear and one in front. We blew a whistle and we charged in and it worked! They were caught totally off guard and we were having a riot. Revenge was sweet!

Then I noticed two or three guys in H Troop were bleeding from their heads and faces. I went to their aid and found out that one of the guys in my troop had lost it and was punching out every face he saw. It turned from a good ragging to a very serious incident. We did what we could to help the injured members, and guys from both troops jumped on the offender while others tried to keep the peace as tempers were boiling over.

The incident set off a powder keg of questions at Depot. Everyone was blaming everyone else. Some thought that it was the fault of the junior ranks, H Troop included, for not following tradition by daring to horse-trough us, the senior troop. Others thought that the instructors incited the circumstances by encouraging recruits to take matters into their own hands. And some thought that it was an isolated incident, the result of us taking our roll as senior troop too far. I don't know why it happened, but one thing was for sure, the RCMP was not going to let it slip by ignored.

Just like we thought we knew horsemanship, we thought we knew how to investigate. That was until we were questioned, like criminals, by the experienced police officers at Depot. The truth was quickly found out and amends needed to be made. The member who pounded out his co-workers was thrown out of the RCMP. The ring leader was allowed to stay, but would not be allowed to attend graduation. The rest of us graduated in our muted brown serge (not the traditional scarlet Red Serge). And, to drive the point home, our ceremony took place in the Drill Hall, outside of public view.

Looking back, I understand now that Depot was a lesson from start to finish. I was expected to push myself until I understood where the upper limits of my abilities were. The instructors were there to make sure I pushed myself so hard that I fell off the horse (or cow, as the case was) and that I pulled myself and my troop mates up out of the muck and got back on the horses. I learned that what I saw as failures at the time were only minor setbacks, and were actually part of a great success.

Bill Perry, my feared drill instructor, became a good friend and was the best man at my wedding. I have many friends from my time in the RCMP. When I left the RCMP after five years to follow other interests, I took the confidence and training the RCMP gave me into my careers as an architect, musician, and Hollywood set designer. Success breeds more success: the success I had at Depot and in the RCMP contributed greatly to the success in other areas of my life. Even though I was only a police officer for a few years, I have been a Mountie my whole life.

DEPOT: A WHOLE NEW WORLD
Constable Joshua Reeves
Chestermere, Alberta

On November 27, 2008, at the young age of twenty-two, I received a phone call that changed my life. When I answered the phone I listened intently, and the first few words made my heart beat harder than it ever had.

"Congratulations! Your application was successful and you'll be going to Depot. Do you accept this offer?" I wondered if I heard right? Could it have been that the college education and all the volunteer work had finally paid off? Did this mean that I would be quitting my job at the local mall and leaving my family behind in Ontario while I went to live in Regina, Saskatchewan for six months? There was a lot, all at once, rushing through my mind.

I told the recruitment staff on the other end of the phone that of course I accept. I became even more excited as we further discussed flight tickets to the training academy and departure dates. This was quickly becoming a reality for me, and I was getting a sinking feeling in the pit of my stomach.

Even though I was excited to begin this journey, I knew I had to break the news to my parents and fiancée. I had to tell them the happy news that I would be going to Depot for training, and the sad news that I would be leaving them for a half of a year. I made this sound as positive as I could, but there was no way of avoiding the many tears shed between my family and me. But deep down, I knew they were happy for me.

On December 14, 2008, I said goodbye to my family at the airport. I had never felt such feelings as the ones I felt that day. I looked at the eyes of my family members with a false smile, already looking at them like strangers, as I knew it would be a completely different life when I saw them again. I kissed my fiancée and felt her quivering arms around me and her tears run down my shoulder. I told her I would call often and time would fly. She told me she would be okay, and I believed she would be after the first week or so.

The three hour flight to Regina was the loneliest I had ever been. I knew that the plane would not turn around for me to have one last moment with my family. I knew I was going to a place where I had never been before, and I would be living among a troop of thirty-two strangers. I was leaving my loved ones behind, and dropping my whole life for this unknown journey. I didn't know what awaited me once off the plane.

Regina was damned cold! When I landed, it was minus fifty-three with the wind chill. I had never felt this kind of cold before. It was accompanied by meeting thirty-one other strangers in the same situation as me. We made small talk, sharing where we were from and talking about what we had gotten ourselves into. We had walked through the doors that thousands of Mounties before us had gone through. The buildings at Depot seemed old, and almost like a prison. The premises were fenced with barb wire, and I always had the feeling that someone was watching me. I learned quickly that before I stepped out of my dorm each morning I had better be in top-shape. You could bet that if I had a wrinkle in my shirt or marched incorrectly, I would be disciplined by being sent to "Learning Assistance Parade"; or "LA", as it was called, among other things, was designed to be an added pressure in your already busy day. The "parade" was really just standing at attention in the Drill Hall with all the other people who got caught, and explaining to a drill instructor why you were sent there (wrinkled shirt, dust on your hat, etc...) and explaining what you did to fix it. The real detraction from LA was that it was a thief of precious time. While your troop mates had the chance to spend those few extra minutes getting organized for the day or cramming in the last of the previous night's homework, you had to explain to another adult the merits of ironing your shirt. After a while it became a game in the troop, to see who would get "caught" and to see how long you could hold out before being sent to LA. Some were sent weekly, some only got sent once or twice in the six months.

Over the following twenty-four weeks, I would go through a roller coaster ride. I would make friends, I would make enemies. I would have moments of pride talking about my accomplishments over the phone with my family, and I would have long sleepless nights reminiscing the feeling of watching my fiancée sleep. I would do incredible things, and would feel incredible pain.

One of the first instances when I felt that I was becoming a police officer was when our troop was given a Crown Victoria to take out for patrols around Regina. This car, which was called Charlie 15, was basically an unmarked police vehicle. It felt awkward to sit behind the wheel. The first time I took Charlie 15 out for a drive I was with one of my good friends I had met at Depot. I drove first. We left the land of Depot and took a ride into downtown Regina. I had never driven a rear-wheel drive vehicle before, and the roads were snow covered and slick.

I turned down a side street that was narrow with cars parked on both sides of it. I was driving at about twenty kilometres per hour, and crossed the centre of the road to drive around a parked vehicle. The vehicle felt as if it was on ice and it started to slide. We slid steadily until we spun a full one hundred and eighty degrees and stopped in the opposite lane, nearly colliding with a parked vehicle. While this was happening in what felt like slow motion: I looked at my partner who was bracing himself with one hand on the dashboard and one hand on the ceiling. He had such a strong look of terror in his eyes. Once we realized the danger was over, we looked at each other and laughed hysterically. At that point in training, to damage a civilian's car and a Depot car on our first outing, we'd be in so much trouble.

Driving rear-wheel drive wasn't my thing. Another time, I pulled into an alley thinking my vehicle could plough through the one-foot deep snow, so I chanced it, and I got stuck in the middle of the alley. It was getting dark, and thankfully there weren't many people around to point and laugh at us, but there were still a couple. We drove our patrols in uniform, with the clear cadet insignia on our shoulders, without firearms or police tools, all of which went to show the public that we weren't police yet. We searched the trunk for the shovel. We began shovelling out the tires, and realized we were stuck pretty badly. Panic began to set in, as we knew it was already getting late. We could get disciplined if we weren't back at Depot before curfew. To make matters worse, a civilian car had pulled up behind us. He just stayed in his vehicle, masked behind the bright headlights. As we were shovelling, we were wondering if this was someone making a YouTube video of two cadets running around like chickens with their heads cut off. Eventually, we were able to get the car unstuck and returned to Depot safely. No sign of the video online, thankfully.

There comes a time at Depot when the cadets are sprayed with OC spray, better known as pepper spray. The purpose of this exercise is to know the effects, and know what to expect when it is deployed. When my turn came, I stood in front of my facilitator. I had closed my eyes as tight as I could, and held my breath. I had felt a steady stream of a gel-like substance cover my face. I had thought to myself, a few seconds later, that it wasn't that bad. I opened my eyes, and that's when things changed...

As the liquid fire ran down into my eyes, it became instant pain. Everything I had in my sinuses and all the saliva in my mouth had started to come out at once. I wondered how my eyes could recover from that kind of pain. Would I go blind? As my troop mate fanned cool air onto my face, it seemed like the pain only got worse. Every pore on my face burned, and I could feel it. The effects wore off about an hour later, and the troop laughed about our ordeal later that evening over a dinner of a dozen pizzas.

I noticed about halfway through training that I really liked it at Depot. I still missed my family, but I was no longer sad. I had lost twenty pounds and was in excellent shape. I had become a trained fighter. I was constantly making sure I was freshly shaven. I was trimming my hair. I made my bed every morning at 5:30 AM and made sure it was wrinkle free. I hung all my clothes in my closet the exact same way. I was proud of who I was. I had become so... military-like.

There came a time when I was noticing the senior troops more often. They had high-brown boots that were polished so nicely that it was a shame they had to be worn. They had red lines on their shoulders, indicating they were graduating soon. I wanted that so badly. It seemed like that day would never come. But soon enough, I had my own high-brown boots. I spent many hours late at night polishing my boots to get the perfect shine. Once I was finished they sparkled and looked great. I had never been interested in boots before, because I thought they were just for cowboys. But my new boots represented my success, and many hours of polishing, so I enjoyed wearing them any chance I had.

It seemed like in a blink of an eye I was being fitted for my Red Serge. I tried it on for the first time and I couldn't believe what I saw. I looked in the mirror for probably fifteen minutes trying to believe my eyes—I looked like a Mountie. This was when I realized that I was almost done my training. I had instant pride while I stared at myself because I had come so far with my dream. I worked hard, for years, for this moment. I walked out of my dorm into the hallway to see the rest of my troop. We had all been wearing our Red Serge and trying it on for the first time together. We all shared the same feeling as we looked each other up and down. It felt like the day before we had just arrived and were all strangers, but we made it to near the end of our training and all seemed so grown-up.

I flew my family out to Regina on June 1, 2009 to watch me graduate, and leave my cadet rank behind as I welcomed my new title as constable. When my fiancée and parents arrived at Depot they laid eyes on me for the first time as I wore my Red Serge. My dad instantly cried, my mother couldn't stop hugging me, and my fiancée was smiling ear to ear so hard that I thought her face would break.

They watched me accept my badge and watched my troop present our marching ceremony. They knew that deep down I was the same person as I was before coming to Depot, but they also knew I had changed. These changes were for the better. I have never felt so alive. I was proud, and I was more ambitious than ever. I left Depot that week, realizing now that the friends I had made there would be scattered all over the country. To this day, in some sick and twisted way, I miss Depot and going through hell each week. Depot had felt like home.

THE PHONE CALL
Constable Aaron White
Dauphin, Manitoba

It was the fifth day of November 2007. I don't remember exactly what time the phone rang, but at the time I was posted to a tiny hamlet in the Arctic called Hall Beach. The days were extremely short and I was, as was the custom during my time in "The Beach", lounging in my robe, all the while trying to housebreak my new yellow lab puppy, Pomme.

In my memory, the phone was louder than usual. Being on call 24/7 gave the phone an already sinister twist, but in my guts it felt different. I recognized the voice on the other end immediately, it was Michel. We had known each other since Depot and he suffered with me as a roommate for eight months while we did our field training.

"Something is wrong in Kimmirut!" Michel exclaimed, "They can't get a hold of Doug." Michel explained that he was in the detachment working and got a courtesy call from someone who knew both Doug and him. He emphasized that it didn't look good.

"Uh-huh," I responded nonchalantly. I knew Kimmirut; I had been there five months earlier for a few weeks. It is a community of about four hundred and fifty people on the southwest corner of Baffin Island. The radios there were terrible. In fact, while I was there I had no radio at all, and had to get in touch with the dispatchers over the phone everyday in the morning, and then at the end of the day to log-off shift. You'd get called out in the middle of the night, make your arrest and call when you got home to let the guardian angels in dispatch know that you were okay. I tried to underline to Michel the need to be patient, but his voice suggested that things may be bigger than the comfort I could give him.

I had forgotten to update dispatch tons of times and suggested that Doug was probably sidetracked with something else. Kimmirut was a small town, but at all times of the day you could expect to find somebody on the street. Sometimes just some kids walking laps, or sometimes a heavily intoxicated male in a canoe by the water. You'd stop and talk to the kids, or try and wake up the family of the guy in the canoe to take care of him, and lose track of time, all the while forgetting to update dispatch. When your only backup is in the passenger seat, and you can only get help by airplane, the radio doesn't strike you as a lifeline. It is, and God bless the dispatchers who stay on the line, but complacency is a constant concern.

I told him to wait for a bit and we'll deal with whatever was going on when we had more details. There was no use speculating. He agreed and we said goodbye. I hung up the phone and my fiancée asked me what was going on. I explained why Michel had called, downplaying my own apprehensions. The North was a small community of officers, and Isabelle knew Doug and Michel too. Isabelle and I continued to talk about the guys from Iqaluit. I told her the story about Doug's first night in Iqaluit, again, and how silly we were.

The new officers in Iqaluit during field training all lived in two apartments across from each other. You stole each other's groceries and then became instant friends. You would spend somewhere between five to eight months together, and would then be shipped to smaller communities. I went to Hall Beach, Michel to Pond Inlet, and Doug went to Kimmirut.

The very first night Doug Scott was in Iqaluit, the roomies all got together in his new apartment and told the largest, most exaggerated stories that brand new Mounties can tell about their six weeks on the job. We were ten-feet-tall and immortal. The stories were getting louder and larger, the doors we kicked in got thicker, they exploded off the hinges, and Doug was getting more and more excited. "That's what I'm here for. That's what I want!" he halfway shouted.

Of course Michel and I played it cool. "Yeah, you'll probably see some of that once you've been on the job for a bit," I explained, as a steely veteran of six weeks. Dougie was going to fit in just fine.

A few weeks later, Doug and I were on patrol together by the airport when we came across a kid on the side of the road with his bike. The chain was off and the kid seemed upset. Dougie jumped out and started to try and fix the bike. It was cold and bitter; I suggested that we just give him a ride home. Doug told me he could fix it and he kept working. After several minutes of extreme cold, the bike was back in working order and the kid was thankful as he went riding off. Doug's small stature grew to eight feet and he gave me a look. "Yeah, yeah superhero, you did good," I responded to his unspoken remark.

As we got back in the truck, the radio came to life asking for someone to take a stolen bicycle complaint. Doug had just fixed the thief's getaway car! I chuckled and felt really good as I returned my own "look".

Of course I didn't praise him at the time, but upon getting back to the detachment I spoke to his field trainer, Jeff, a friend of mine and Doug's, and told him the part about fixing the bike. I left out the fact that it was stolen. I saw Jeff's pride swell at the thought of Doug fixing bikes while wearing his forge cap in the cold.

Back in Hall Beach, my phone rang again. I expected this to be the call letting me know that Doug had his radio turned off and everything was fine. I'd remember to ride him about that the next time I saw him.

"Dougie's dead, Aaron," Michel's voice cracked on the phone.

I sat immediately at my dinner table. "What?" I responded.

"He's gone. I don't know what happened yet, but he's gone." I couldn't get off the phone quick enough. This was stupid. How could Michel know that? But he wouldn't let me hang up until I understood. We talked about what was to happen next, and asked each other over and over again how we were taking the news and if we were okay. I tried not to cry, but didn't quite make it. Eventually there was nothing else to be said, Michel and I said goodnight.

I sat at the dinner table quiet, looking at the phone. Isabelle was on the couch and asked me, "What's going on?"

The simplicity of the question incensed me for a moment and I said, "Doug's dead." Isabelle's instant tears softened me and I cried as well. This was a new experience for Isabelle. She had only been in the world of cops for a few months and she hadn't experienced that kind of loss.

We talked quietly for a few hours about what to do next and soon it was early morning. We went to bed for a few hours before I had to get up. I had breakfast, put my uniform and my gun on, and I went to work, as did Doug's other Mountie friends. There was one else to go, so we would have to mourn later.

THE CITY SLICKER MEETS HER MATCH
Sergeant Mia Poscente
Toronto, Ontario

I like to consider myself adaptable, self-sufficient, and clever enough to maneuver through tricky and challenging situations. I have talked my way out of confrontations both as an undercover operator and as a uniformed police officer. With almost twenty years of policing experience, I've seen it all. Right? Not so fast. While some locals actually believe Toronto is the centre of the universe, I am at least open-minded enough to admit I could learn a thing or two and expand my experiences. That is precisely why an opportunity to work for a month in a remote, fly-in, First Nations reserve in Manitoba was so appealing to me.

I arrived by RCMP plane (and I got to sit in the co-pilot seat!) in a rain storm, landing on a grass and gravel airstrip. Jack, the detachment commander, greeted me and led me to the waiting RCMP truck, then boat. With all my gear, I sat at the front of a boat and was pelted by ice as we bounced across Family Lake and through the channel to Little Grand Rapids, which would be my home until mid-October. It is much colder in Manitoba in September than it is in Toronto, and I questioned myself for volunteering to do this.

The next day was warmer, and after a crash course in driving the boat, Jack dropped the keys to the detachment in my hand and took off for his well-deserved vacation. Did I mention I had never driven a boat before? But really, how hard could it be? After all, it was a wide open body of water and there was nothing to hit.

I spent the next several weeks driving a truck and a quad, learning about life on a reserve and dealing with its unique policing challenges, and actively avoiding having to drive the boat. There were two boats, actually. The big boat (the one I learned to drive) had a one hundred and fifty-five engine (whatever that means), and the smaller boat had a ninety. The water levels were dropping drastically and were apparently at the lowest levels ever seen by the locals. Rocks were sticking out of the water that had never even been mapped. At the RCMP dock on "the other side" (where we had to go to get mail, go to the Northern Store, and the airport) the water was less than a foot deep, making it extremely difficult to dock. Evan, an experienced boater, had even grounded the ninety and had to get in the water to push it out (while the rest of us sat in the boat, he was the junior guy after all). The one hundred and fifty-five was too big and could no longer be used.

After a terrible snow storm (yes, in early October) that stranded several members both incoming and outgoing, we got up bright and early one Saturday morning to get everyone where they needed to be. Snow covered the boats as we prepared for the first of two trips across the lake. The sun was coming up and the intense autumn colours were made brilliant by the glistening frost. The lake was like glass, all remnants of the horrific winds gone. Steam rose from the water in areas where the warmth of the sun touched down.

This was to be my day of reckoning: I had to drive the boat by myself back from the other side. As we got into the ninety for the first trip, Evan asked if I wanted to drive. "No, you go ahead," I replied, not wanting to have to dock in the shallow water with witnesses. He drove across the pristine water effortlessly and brought the boat to a smooth stop along the dock, facing out to make it easier for me to pull away. I retrieved the truck from the garage and drove the first group to the airport, returning to the dock alone. "It's just you and me," I said aloud to myself as I started the boat engine. I had watched closely as other members pulled out, so I knew what to do. I dropped the engine very slowly as I crept away from the dock. Once away from the rocks and into deeper water, I dropped it a bit more and pushed down on the throttle. The nose of the boat went up, as expected, and I repeated what Jack told me in my boat-driving lesson a month earlier.

"Turn the steering wheel back and forth to bring the nose down then open 'er up. If the nose doesn't come down, trim up," was what Jack said.

Prior to this I thought "trim" was what you did when your hair was a bit too long, but now I knew it was also a reference to raising or lowering the outboard motor on a boat. Look at me using lingo! I opened 'er up and the nose went up, so I trimmed up, then the nose went up some more, so I turned the wheel back and forth, but the nose didn't come down. I couldn't see the water over the front of the boat, except when I smashed down onto it. Over and over, up in the air with the engine roaring so loud I could actually hear it echoing off the distant trees. Then SMASH down onto the water, then RRRNNNMMM up in the air—my feet came off the deck and as I held onto the steering wheel I felt like a flag waving in the wind. "Don't let goooooooo!" I screamed in my head, unable to reach the throttle to slow down. I bounced the boat off the water about ten times before the engine finally conked out and I drifted to a stop in a circle of wake. But further out the water remained like glass, and I became perplexed by how calm the water was out there, yet how rough it was where I was driving. I remained calm by reminding myself that it was fresh water and there were no sharks.

"Okay," I said to myself, "remember what Jack said: put it in neutral, start the engine and get going again." I did, and it worked. So I started cutting through the water again. Up came the nose and I turned the steering wheel back and forth, and I trimmed up, and I opened 'er up and RRRNNNMMM—SPLASH—RRRNNNMMM—SPLASH, over and over and again and again, all the way across the lake. I came through the channel toward our dock doing a wheelie with the boat, and as I slowed down, a huge wake I had caused swept past the boat, swamping the dock where the remaining three people stood in silence, awestruck no doubt by the spectacle before them. I carefully docked the boat and stepped out, doing my best to conceal my shaking legs, as someone took the rope and tied it off. Together, and in complete silence, we loaded up and all got back in the boat. "Want me to drive?" George said quietly.

"Sure," I replied.

And in complete silence he drove across the pristine water effortlessly, and brought the boat to a smooth stop along the dock, facing out to make it easier for me to pull away. Still without a word spoken, we all got out of the boat and loaded everything onto the truck. There wasn't room for all of us in the cab, so two of us would have to ride in the back. I hopped into the truck bed, as did Ann-Marie, with whom I had become good friends. As the truck doors closed and we went out of hearing from the others, she broke the silence by turning to me and demanding, "What the hell was that?"

Having as close to a complete meltdown as I have ever had in my life, I sobbed, "I couldn't get the nose down on the boat!"

"No kidding," she chided. "We could hear you from across the frickin' lake! You came around the corner like this (motioning with her hand almost straight up in the air). What were you doing?"

"Jack said to trim up to get the nose down!" I pleaded in my defense.

"On the one-fifty-five! On the ninety you have to trim *down* to get the nose down!" she said with exasperation.

"How was I supposed to know that?" I cried.

"Well it's all over now," she consoled me. "Pull yourself together and whatever you do, just don't show weakness to the guys!"

With that we had a good laugh and I realized I wasn't as rugged as I thought I was. I could laugh at myself and with my friends. This would be one of those stories that I would tell over and over again. But, unlike "the fish that got away", I wouldn't have to embellish because there were witnesses!

Order up the "I survived a month in Little Grand Rapids" T-shirt and get me back home!

HAITI
Constable Pierre Robitaille
Hamilton, Ontario

These events took place during my second United Nations (UN) mission
in Haiti in 2005 (I was also there in 1995). The aim for both missions
was to help form a modern national police force by teaching and mentoring all levels of the Haitian National Police (HNP), and help to protect the
fragile democracy that existed there. The one difference, since I was there
in 1995, was that the presidency of Jean-Bertrand Aristide had brought in
loads of weapons which he thought were somehow going to help him keep
power. He distributed these arms to the poor slums of Port au Prince. By
2005, Aristide had been ousted, but the weapons remained, causing terrible havoc and devastation to the impoverished country: assassinations,
kidnappings, home invasions, and tortures were all consequences of that
asinine strategy. During my slated time for this mission, we were told that
presidential elections were to take place sometime in the fall and the elections were a priority to the UN mission.

I was paired with a young constable from the Quebec City Police. Eric
was eager and enthusiastic about being part of a UN mission in a foreign
country; he could not wait to get to the area assigned to us and start mentoring the local police.

Eric and I headed for the regional command of Petit Goave, which
comprised the communities of Leogane, Grand Goave, and Petit Goave.
Upon our arrival we learned that the UN Civilian Police (UNCIVPOL)
regional commander had made it a priority for all the CIVPOLS to look
after the presidential elections. On a daily basis we'd visit census/electoral
offices where we'd collect the number of people who were registering with
those offices located in different cities, towns, and villages. To abide by the
UN mandate, another priority was to regularly count the number of pris-

oners kept in jail and identify if there were human rights abuses. It was very frustrating for Eric and me to have so little interaction with the members of the HNP, but we had to abide by the instructions coming from our regional commander. Some of our colleagues were so disappointed that they had applied for transfers out of the region.

On September 26, 2005, after gathering the required information from the census/electoral office in Leogane, Eric and I attended the HNP office to collect the number of prisoners and find out the reasons for their incarcerations. It was around 10:00 AM when we arrived at the commissariat in Leogane, where we were asked by one of Leogane HNP senior investigators if we could help them with a serious investigation. One of the local lawyers, Maitre (Me.) Philippe Joseph, had sent a letter addressed to the Sri Lankan UN camp (military peacekeepers) regarding the alleged murder of a family in the area, about one hour away by vehicle in the mountains. Me. Joseph had sent the information to the UN because he did not have confidence in the HNP, the letter stated this fact. In turn, the Sri Lankans had assigned a patrol led by Captain Rodrigo to bring the matter to the attention of the HNP and to further investigate. The HNP had already sent someone looking for Me. Joseph.

As we stood there discussing the letter, I saw him approaching. He was a typical Haitian professional who was trying his best to improve the conditions and living standards of Haitian life. He was well respected.

He first spoke with the HNP investigators in Creole, which I partially understood. Then in French, he told us what the whole story was about. It concerned people that he had previously helped to try and resolve a land dispute with between their neighbour, but had failed to bring the parties to an agreement. The day before a young boy had come to him. He was crying and very frightened, and he had told Me. Joseph that he was with the Godin family when a gang of *chimeres* (miscreants) had come for them, and, after a short argument, they started beating Mr. Godin, his wife, his fifteen-year-old daughter, and the boy himself, who was a friend of the family. The child bore the obvious marks of some hard hitting, but he managed to escape and had watched from faraway as the family was murdered. He did not know where to turn when someone told him about Me. Joseph. The boy said they had buried the bodies on a hill.

Me. Joseph tried to keep him close by, offering him a place to stay for the night, but the boy was so scared he left. The next morning, with the help of others, Me. Joseph had searched for the young boy but without success. He had just vanished, scared for his life. He knew if the group of thugs found him he would be killed.

The HNP asked us if we could go search for the bodies with them. Eric and I looked at each other, finally something to justify the reason for us to be in that country. The HNP were a little surprised that we were so eager to help. We knew they asked us to help because they did not have a vehicle to take them to that location, as they would have had to drive in a river bed and go through water knee deep or even deeper. If it was not for us, it would take them the better part of a day to get where they needed to go.

So the ever smiling young Captain Rodrigo and his crew, the two HNP investigators, Me. Joseph, Eric and I would go look for the bodies. At Me. Joseph's suggestion, we stopped at the court in Leogane to advise a justice of the peace (acting as a coroner) of the strong possibility that we were dealing with multiple murders. The justice took the necessary courts dispositions and requested to come along with an assistant. Since we had room in our vehicle we agreed to bring them with us. We joined the Sri Lankans at their camp on the way out of town. They had gone ahead of us to get two shovels and gloves for digging. With a truck full of people and supplies, we were off on our quest.

We first travelled east and then left the paved road for a dirt path heading south. We followed a row of tall trees that led us into the bed of a large river. For many small villages, including our destination, the river bed was the fastest and most manageable way to access the isolated communities. So it was in-and-out of water and often waiting for our Sri Lankan companions, who were driving an under-powered truck compared to our Nissan Patrol work-horse.

It took the better part of an hour to get close to where the murder was supposed to have taken place. We couldn't go any further with our vehicles, so we left them with two soldiers and started walking up the steep river embankment. After twenty minutes of trekking through the mountains we found a spot, close to the landmark given to Me. Joseph, where it was obvious that someone had recently dug a big hole.

The two soldiers removed their helmets and flak jackets, put on gloves, and started digging. Eric and I took turns helping them and Captain Rodrigo also jumped in to assist.

Eerily, we had not seen any locals since leaving our vehicle. Usually, whenever and wherever a group of *blancs* (strangers) from the UN would show up so would the local people, sniffing around for anything we might give them, be it candy, food, water, and the like. This time everybody stayed away; they knew very well what we were looking for and nobody wanted any part of it.

After about twenty minutes of digging we got to hard dirt. Also, it did not feel or smell like what we were searching for. Me. Joseph, the court crew, and an investigator went to inquire at some of the houses, attempting to find out if someone would talk, but the locals were all afraid. Finally, Me. Joseph found someone who told him that what we were looking for was a little further up the hill. Within minutes we found another location where the soil had been disturbed and we resumed digging. It did not take long to realize that this also was not the location of the grave. We walked further atop another little hill and found a larger area which had obviously been dug recently. This time we could all sense that a horrible event had taken place.

It was now 12:30 PM, the sun was directly above us, the ninety-plus degree temperature with the ninety-eight percent humidity was hardly bearable, but those small, wiry soldiers laid down their equipment once more and started digging. Again, Eric and I took our turn with the shovels. We (the Sri Lankans and Eric and I) noticed that the Haitians didn't help with the digging.

I brought two, one and a half litre bottles of water. I drank one and gave the other to the HNPs and the court personnel. I would later really miss that water.

Before too long I could smell the foul stench of death and, with each shovelful of dirt taken out, the smell got stronger. Captain Rodrigo was digging and found what appeared to be a leg. We were careful to make sure we did not damage the body. Twenty minutes later the body of the young girl was taken out of the hole. Right away one of the HNP investigators called her name—he knew her. When we removed her body from the hole, we saw part of another body underneath, but it was covered with a heavy rock. It took some work to move the rock away from the body of Mr. Godin. We weren't able to ascertain the cause of death at the scene so an autopsy would be required.

Part way through removing the bodies I felt completely drained, exhausted by the heat, the effort, and the walk. But we owed it to the victims to take their bodies out of the dirt, to continue the investigation, and to bring the murderers to justice. Under Mr. Godin, we found the corpse of his wife, and again all we could do was to speculate on the cause of death.

Almost two hours after finding the grave and plenty of hard work by Captain Rodrigo, his two soldiers, Eric and me, we had the three bodies out in the open for the justice of the peace to review. He dictated a few things to his assistant but never even came close to the bodies—neither did Me. Joseph nor the HNPs. They were all speaking Creole. I think they were talking about what to do next. I was exhausted and light headed.

This was a *paysan* (peasant) family. They had a hard life, no doubt, with Mr. Godin farming what he could from his small plot of land, with his wife and daughter walking the long distance to Leogane to sell what they had left for a few *gourdes* (Haitian money) to buy what else they needed. The toils of their lives were seen in Mr. Godin's large, rough hands and the svelte physique of his family, but it was their lives, theirs to enjoy together.

We had to make arrangements to bring the bodies to Leogane for autopsies, and try to find the young boy who witnessed the murders. We also had to find out if we were at the actual murder scene or if the killings took place somewhere else. We had looked around for possible weapons and traces of blood but to no avail. We also had to find out if there were any other witnesses, and hopefully identify and apprehend the suspects. We already had a few names provided to Me. Joseph by the young boy. We thought that we may have a few weeks of work ahead of us.

Right away I sensed a problem when we suggested to the HNP that they stay to keep continuity of the bodies. This is policing 101: once police officers come in contact with evidence, they don't lose control of the evidence for fear of it being tampered with or losing it. The HNP refused to stay with the bodies and so did the court people and Me. Joseph, saying that it was unsafe for anyone to remain behind, that the killers might still be around. It was unpractical for us or the Sri Lankan soldiers to stay behind. Plus, we were blancs and probably would be out of the country when and if this matter went to trial.

All we could do was assist the HNP as much as possible but the investigation was theirs, not ours. We had to figure out what we could do with the corpses. We did not have the equipment or enough room to bring them to Leogane. We looked for people to keep watch over the bodies but it was impossible to find anyone, they were all afraid.

We had to get to the morgue and bring back help and equipment to move the corpses to the morgue. It took us over an hour to return to where we left the court personnel and the HNP. The HNP were to make arrangements for the morgue personnel to accompany us back to the gravesite. We went to the Sri Lankan's camp where I finally could drink some fresh water and refill my bottle. Water never tasted so good.

Close to an hour later, a truck from the *Morgue Ange du Ciel* and two attendants arrived at the Sri Lankan camp with the HNPs. Their truck sure had seen better days. The HNPs jumped in our vehicle and we left followed by Captain Rodrigo, his patrol, and the truck from the morgue.

On the way back to the gravesite, not only did the soldiers have to push their own vehicle, but also the truck from the morgue. Eric and I thought that it would never make it, but with lots of help it did—I even jumped out and pushed a few times. We finally got back to the location on the river and hurried up to the gravesite in time to see that a few pigs were dangerously close to the bodies. The soldiers picked up rocks and were successful in chasing them away; thankfully the bodies had not been disturbed.

The employees of the morgue had brought one stretcher. While look-ing at the corpses, they talked amongst themselves. It didn't look good. I could understand very little of what they were saying, but the gist was that they refused to take the bodies: something about the fact that they had been dead for too long and the stench was terrible. Trying to convince them otherwise was futile. Captain Rodrigo looked at us with an air of resignation. Eric and I were appalled and we made it known.

Looking at the HNP investigators, it started to sink in for me. We were telling them that autopsies were needed for successful prosecution, but in these parts of the world, where the law is still based on old principles of the Napoleonic Code, convictions do not rely on evidence obtained dur-ing autopsies, and hospitals are too busy dealing with the living. Also, who would have paid for the autopsies? The HNP did not have funds for that nor did anyone else. Moreover, the HNP in Leogane, as in other commis-sariats, were way under strength. They only had one vehicle and it was in dire need of repair.

A major operation would be needed to apprehend the suspects. Peo-ple on the mountain would not help the HNP because in those parts of the country they knew that the HNP could not protect them: justice had "short arms", and was not applied the same way as in Canada. Voudou, black magic, and lynching mobs are feared the most, and in this case it cost the Godin family their lives. It is reminiscent of the "law of the jungle" or the Wild West where people with power can "rule the roost". The HNP would simply have to wait to apprehend the suspects when and if they saw them around the city of Leogane.

When we came back to our regional post we wrote a long report detailing the events of the day and the confirmed murders. A further report was sent to our CIVPOL headquarters, trying to muster some help from the Serious Crime section in Port au Prince but to no avail, they were swamped having to deal with their own difficulties.

I would often think about the family and how their lives had ended, and I would inquire with the HNP about new developments in the case, but for them it never attracted their attention again. Eric got transferred about one month later and my duties increased with the nearing of the presidential election. In conversation with Me. Joseph, who I would often see, even taking part in his radio show, I would ask him about the case but he preferred not to talk about it. I think he was spooked by the crime and wanted to put it all behind him.

Rebuilding from the devastating earthquake of January 12, 2010 might have provided lots of work around Port au Prince and in the southwest region of the country. But, it will take many more mega projects to take the country out of its present situation. Hope for change in the country of Haiti rests with its young people and their thirst for studying and learning. Only about ten percent of children get educated, because families don't have the money to send their children to school. Free education is the cornerstone of progress: it is what will take Haiti out of its misery and lead it into a successful future, and it should be the focus, in my opinion, of the mission in Haiti. Educate the present generation and twenty years from now you will see radical change.

I went to Haiti to pay it forward to the Haitian people, in particular to the Haitian-Canadians who have played a big part in my life. Many of my secondary school teachers were from Haiti: most of them had escaped during the Papa Doc tyrannical era. My Latin and philosophy teacher walked with an obvious limp because he had been tortured by the *tonton-macoutes*; he was accused of being a communist. His wife, who later held a post in the Haitian government, had taught my sister. I was also grateful to another Haitian, Doctor Pierre Benjamin, a cardiologist whose contribution kept my father alive for seven more years after he had suffered a massive heart attack. For me, it was a small sacrifice, and why I went twice. Security, health, and education are at the forefront of Canada's values: those Haitian teachers and doctors came to Canada years ago attracted by these values.

Teaching our values every day by talking to Haitians about how things are done in Canada and working with them remain our best contributions to the UN mission.

Haiti *chérie*. One day I will return.

THE ISLAND LAKE EXPERIENCE
Constable Xavier Pilon
Island Lake, Manitoba

Island Lake is a remote area located in Manitoba, approximately six hundred kilometres northeast of Winnipeg. It is accessible only by aircraft from spring to fall, and by a network of ice roads during four to six weeks in winter. The local RCMP detachment serves a population of approximately ten thousand, living in four First Nation reserves and a handful of Metis settlements. Three of the reserves are located around Island Lake; a one hundred kilometre long, sixty kilometre wide body of water that is home to about thirty-four hundred islands. A fourth reserve is situated one hundred kilometres to the northeast of Island Lake, on the shores of Red Sucker Lake.

The detachment is located on Stevenson Island, a kilometre from the north shore of Island Lake. The Island Lake Detachment maintains a fleet of five boats, several all-terrain vehicles (ATVs), snowmobiles, and four-by-four trucks. Boating is a way of life for the population of Island Lake, and boats are essential to local Mounties for answering calls for service. During more than six months every year, boats are the only practical means of transportation for us to attend the ever-growing communities we police and, hence, to fulfill our commitment to the population we serve. Our detachment is unique in that way.

Boats are not only a way for us to respond to calls for service in different areas of Island Lake; they are used for patrols, prisoner escorts, and, more importantly, marine rescue.

On a stormy, mid-August night in 2010, Constable Erdman Wiebe and I finished our shift at 2:00 AM. We both logged out of the telecommunication system, and dispatchers were advised that I could be reached at home, as usual, until the next morning if an emergency was reported overnight.

I was awakened at 4:15 AM by our dispatchers. A distress call had just been received at the telecommunication centre regarding an air-ambulance crew working in the area. Dispatchers advised me that a pair of air-ambulance technicians, a local medical boat pilot, and a male patient on a stretcher were stranded in their boat on Island Lake, somewhere between Stevenson Island and Garden Hill, the closest reserve. Little information was available, as the stranded party was unaware of their exact location and no phone number or other means of communication were available to reach them. The medical condition of the patient was unknown but it was serious enough to need an airlift to Winnipeg.

I immediately called my partner Erdman at home and we met up at the detachment, located just a few kilometres from our cabins. Rain was pouring down hard, the wind was blowing strong, and waves were as high as we had ever seen them. It was pitch-dark outside. We quickly brainstormed a plan of action, gathered extra life jackets, and headed out to the boat-house in the cold rain. By the time we got there, we were already soaked through, but adrenaline and commitment diverted our thoughts.

We opted for our biggest, most stable, and most powerful boat for the operation. We took a few precious but necessary minutes to verify all systems were functioning properly on the boat and fired it up. Then, as I took command of the boat and turned it around to face the raging waters of the lake, we realized this operation would not be as easy as we thought. The inclement weather made the sky so dark even the high-power spotlight of our boat failed to help us see further than our bow. But what else could we do? People were out there, probably cold and drenched and more than likely scared; something had to be done to help them. The decision was easy for Erdman and me: we had to somehow locate the stranded crew and their patient and get them back to safety as soon as possible.

We idled along the route we knew medical crews typically use to travel between Stevenson Island and Garden Hill. No sign of a boat or the people. Our biggest concern at that point was that we wouldn't see objects or people on the lake and might collide with them. We opted on the safe side and chose to travel as slowly as the boat would allow us. As we were getting closer to Garden Hill, we realized no boat was between us and the medical dock on the shore of the reserve. The medical boat had either drifted with the waves and wind or the crew had gotten lost somewhere between nearby islands. As we were scanning our surroundings, Erdman noticed a very bright, flashing light to our left, which appeared to be from a fire truck at the north end of Garden Hill. We couldn't believe the medical boat could have drifted that far. But since we had not yet located it, we thought we would take a closer look at the source of the light.

Island Lake is known to be very dangerous for boaters who are in-experienced with the area, due to hidden reefs and rocks very close to the surface of its waters. One could be cruising at high-speed on open water in an unknown area of the lake and, all of a sudden, collide with a shallow reef, with people and boats possibly being injured. The large number of small islands on the lake makes nighttime travel treacherous, as it is ex-tremely difficult to see some of the islands and reefs, and deviating only a few metres from a safe route can result in a collision.

As we were approaching the flashing light, we realized it was actually originating from an object located on the lake, between the north point of Stevenson Island and an island known as Wass Island, located approxi-mately two kilometres to the northwest of Stevenson. We idled towards the light and confirmed it was the boat that we were looking for. One of the medical technicians was standing in the middle of the boat holding an emergency beacon.

All four occupants were drenched, cold, and obviously very happy to see us. The patient had been removed from his stretcher for safety reasons and he said he was capable of walking. He was immediately transferred into our boat, followed by the rest of the stranded crew.

In the warmth of the enclosed cabin of our patrol boat, the driver of the medical boat explained that he had experienced technical difficulties with the boat's motor. Unable to use the motor, the crew and their boat drifted approximately three kilometres west before they found themselves caught against a shallow reef. They tried contacting several local phone numbers for help, but finally called the Mounties as they could not get help from anyone else.

By the time the distressed boaters were rescued, the sun had started to rise, the rain had stopped, and the wind had calmed down. It appeared to us that this was a successful rescue and we were all satisfied everyone would make it safely to shore. But an unexpected electrical problem with our patrol boat suddenly left us powerless, less than fifteen metres from the north shore of Stevenson Island. Erdman and I attempted to locate the source of the problem but we were unable to get the motor started again.

We had no choice but to call in another member to reach us with a second boat and tow us to shore. I called Constable Dan Rouleau and explained to him the situation we had gotten ourselves into. He told me he would meet us right away with a second patrol boat.

But we realized we were drifting to shore. I called Dan back and told him what we might need was not a second boat but rather a truck, as we were about to make shore close to a local convenience store on Stevenson Island. He met us with a truck at the store where our boat landed only a few metres from a dock. Erdman and I jumped off the boat and decided that we had to move the ten thousand pound behemoth (plus passengers) to the dock as it was unsafe for our passengers to get off on the rocky shore. We first tried pushing it away from the shore so we'd be able to float it to the nearby dock but it was stuck in rocks. As I started pulling the boat towards me into deeper water to free it from the rocks, I quickly found myself pushed by the boat and swimming in full uniform, holding onto the hull as Erdman, in water only to his waist as he is much taller than I, helped me manhandle the boat to the dock. We safely got our passengers to shore. They were able to easily step out of the boat and walk to the police truck.

This is only one example of the many challenges we constantly face in northern, remote, and isolated communities as police officers. We often have to rely on local resources, personal knowledge, and common sense to get the job done, as we don't have access to all the resources normally available in southern and less isolated communities. Strong partnerships with local agencies and community members must be established. Members must be resourceful and use their general knowledge, sometimes even their imaginations, to solve problems. Receiving an emergency call in the middle of the night, with little information to work with, in a place where quickly driving to the location of the problematic situation is not an option can sometimes be frustrating. As much as we are eager to help people in distress, knowing we cannot get there immediately can be nerve-racking and quick-thinking is necessary. A strong bond between Force members and other partners is very important in order to solve problems. The right people must be contacted and good communication must be established. A good knowledge of our equipment and geographical area is also necessary.

The patient was successfully airlifted out for treatment and later returned to the community. After towing our boat and assessing it with a local mechanic, we found out it had failed due to a hidden electrical breaker that we didn't even know was there. Safe to say, everyone at the detachment now knows about that breaker.

After this adventure Erdman and I enjoyed a few hours of sleep, as our uniforms and equipment dried out, before starting another night shift at the end of the day.

Isolation is not for everyone. But I have developed strong relationships with the other members and the team has become an extended family. Living in such a community, as difficult as it can sometimes be, has been a tremendous life experience rich in both personal and cultural experiences. Simply put, this life is for me.

DEPLOYED
Constable Aaron Sheedy
Toronto, Ontario

By virtue of being the RCMP, we're almost always involved in major events (like the Olympics or G20), and this is for several reasons: our sheer numbers, the fact that we're already tasked with protecting the prime minister, the governor general, and other internationally protected people (known as IPPs, such as royalty, foreign heads of state, the pope). Plus, across the country, we have the largest pool of trained Tactical Troop members (crowd management/riot squad), the largest pool of language skills, and the largest pool of Emergency Response Members (SWAT). We have helicopters, boats, ATVs, motorcycles, cars, plus members on skis, bicycles, and even in scuba gear. The list goes on. All in all, we can put on quite the road show, and we have significant experience in managing large deployments.

My role in major events is tied to the Tactical Troop from Toronto. After several years on the troop I feel like a summit roadie. I've followed shows like the "the three amigos" (Prime Minister Stephen Harper, President George W. Bush, and President Felipe Calderon) and the Francophone Summit around the country with fanatic devotion. Of course, it includes the President Obama visit, the Vancouver Olympics, and the G20 in Toronto.

These deployments allow for a break from our usual duties. And, the duties assigned at a major deployment can often have nothing to do with your usual job. My normal job is to investigate international drug importations. But on deployment I can be on foot looking for open booze in public or standing static security outside a hotel and ushering presidential motorcades in and out. For one assignment, we were brought on to the site in a massive hovercraft. You can never really anticipate what is going to happen on deployment.

There was one situation during the Francophone Summit deployment in Quebec City that came to be known as "The crazy cabbie" incident. We were coming back from a night off during the summit via cab to our hotel. We were in plain clothes, but it is hard to believe that the crazy cab driver didn't think we were cops: we were all Section One of the Tactical Troop, the largest members on the troop. There was about a thousand pounds of Mountie stuffed in the cab, all looking cop-like.

During the week before the summit, motorcades were getting to know their prescribed routes and were a common sight in town. As we approached a motorcade on the highway the crazy cab driver said, "These guys don't like it when you pass them."

"No," I said. "I can't imagine that they do."

The crazy cab driver proceeded to roll up to the motorcade but didn't pass; he matched the speed of the procession in the left hand lane. This made the Mounties in the motorcade nervous, not to mention the Mounties in the cab. One of the motorcade cars started to edge over into the crazy cabbie's lane.

"Ah, I think we should go on through," I said.

But rather than speed on through, the crazy cabbie rolled down the passenger window (beside me) and pointed his finger, like a gun, out as far as his arm would reach towards the protected limo and screamed, "BANG! BANG! BANG! BANG!" pretending to shoot at the motorcade!

I don't think David Copperfield could make four Section One Mounties disappear in a moving cab, but we did. The three in the back dove for the floor like it was a World War Two foxhole and I melted myself into the post where the front door closes to the frame and we waited for the hail of bullets to come through the cab, while I devised a plan to grab the wheel if the cabbie got shot. Thankfully, the Mounties in the motorcade either didn't see the incident or saw it for what it was, no shots were fired and the crazy cabbie sped on through.

Also, at the Francophone Summit deployment there was the Charles incident. Charles is a member of the Ontario Tactical Troop, and speaks with a noticeable accent. During international summits, on his time off, Charles has been known to walk up and start a conversation with unsuspecting, uniformed Mounties. The one I witnessed went like this:

"Hello, my name is Charles," said Charles in his thickest of accents.

"I am Corporal Simpson," responded the unsuspecting Mountie.

"I like Canada very much," said Charles.

"I am glad to hear that. We're happy you're here," said Simpson.

"I would like to *stay*," said Charles.

"There is a lot to see here, it is a big country."

"No, no. I would like to stay. I would like to defect," said Charles.

"What?" said Simpson.

"I would like to defect to Canada. You can help me, yes?"

The colour drained from Corporal Simpson's face at the thought of the colossal mess this would cause. He was just standing on the street guarding a door; they didn't cover political defection in his briefing. The relief on Simpson's face when Charles showed him his badge was priceless.

On deployment, one of the biggest questions for everyone is accommodations. There have been a wide variety of digs over the years but none quite like during the deployment at Montebello, Quebec, where the entire troop was put up in a swanky resort with hot tubs in each room and five star dining. We did actually work during that summit: we rode on a hovercraft in full riot gear, hauled our whole troop up a massive hill, and worked in a tear gas-soaked environment. But what is most memorable was the tennis, soccer, and the fine dining in our off hours. We felt as if we were getting away with something and that someone would be along any minute to end the party. It all evens out though. Since then we have stayed in everything from tents, to cots, to cruise ships. A lot of the time you're so happy to see a bed, you don't care.

In February 2010, for seventeen days, the twenty-first Winter Olympiad played out in Vancouver and Whistler, British Columbia. This was the largest deployment that the RCMP had ever mounted. The event hosted over twenty-five hundred elite athletes who competed in fifteen sports in over eighty-five medal events. In addition to the multiple events at multiple venues running at the same time, there was a slew of IPPs coming in and out of the Olympic Theater, as it was called. As well, there was a full-time crowd management concern in downtown Vancouver, as hockey games (sometimes three a day) were ushered in and out of Canada Hockey Place (GM Centre), and the throngs of people coming and going to the nightly medal ceremony at BC Place. Adding to this, the Olympic attractions enticed thousands and thousands of people to take in the sights every day. There were around-the-block lineups to get into The Bay just to buy an Olympic T-shirt or sweater (or mascot or Olympic maple syrup or anything they could stamp the Olympic logo on and put up for sale). And further, there were people voicing their concerns over the costs, the corporate globalization, the eco footprint, and the like that come with the Olympic Games. There were also the other protestors who made use of the crowds and media to get their message some airtime. And, unfortunately, there was the criminal element that took the opportunity to maraud with protest groups and start fights, damage vehicles, turn over mailboxes, and damage property. Thankfully, the tolerance for these people was low and the legitimate protestors were quick to distinguish themselves from these factions.

All of this had to be secured. The RCMP provided the largest contingent, but there were police and support personnel deployed from all over Canada, including deployments from the Canadian Coast Guard, the Canada Border Services Agency, Canadian Forces, and pretty much every other Canadian enforcement agency imaginable. The work done by the Vancouver City Police and Mounties stationed in the Vancouver area was outstanding. Those of us coming from outside British Columbia would have been lost without them.

All told, there were over six thousand security personnel deployed for between two and six weeks over the games. This is in addition to the couple hundred who had been planning the security details for years. The Olympic deployment was so large, so dynamic, and so layered it is hard to fathom what happened, all told.

I lived on the Carnival cruise ship *Elation* during my time at the Olympics. I was bunking with another Section One Mountie and we're both pretty big guys. When we saw our room we walked back into the hallway in disbelief and laughed: it was so small that only one of us could be standing in the room at a time. We pulled back the curtain over the window to see that there actually was no window, sparking another round of disbelieving laughter. We were better off than most because we were able to pick our roommates, but we both bought raffle tickets that, if we won, would give us a private luxury suite. We didn't win but, we're still friends so it worked out okay.

I found life, "on a boat going nowhere" (as Tammy Marshall describes it) challenging. After a couple of weeks, the restrictive arrival and departure procedures, the close quarters, and the world's worst coffee really started to wear on me.

On one of my days off, I got to see Clara Hughes win a bronze medal in the woman's five thousand metre speed skating finals. So there I was, screaming like a mad man, with thousands of others, for Clara, Kristina, and Cindy to leave it all on the ice in deafening waves of cheering as they circled the Richmond Oval at blistering speeds. Amidst the eruption of pure joy and patriotism, as it became clear that Clara medaled, it became clear to me that the Olympics weren't about bad coffee or cruise ships, they were about the greatest athletes in the world coming to the freest country in the world to inspire us. And my job was to let it happen, to let freedom permeate. That was my personal commitment to the Olympics and why I am proud to put my name, in a small way, on the 2010 Winter Olympics. It was the longest and most dynamic event to which I have been deployed.

Now with the G8 and G20 in Toronto behind us, it appears the long stretch of deployments are over. In the past three years, we have been deployed to six major events with significant training commitments in between. Right now the usual routine is welcome. But, as I go about my usual policing duties, I keep an eye on the news for summit announcements, major visits, or protests that might garner the attention of the Tactical Troop, and my oversized tact-bag sits packed and ready to go when the call comes.

THE LITTLE INDIAN THAT COULD
Constable Param Dhillon
Toronto, Ontario

I remember the day I was posted to D Division, and, as all RCMP cadets know, you're not getting your first choice. I recall going to the library at Depot and desperately looking for the town of Fisher Branch on a map of Manitoba. I soon discovered that my career was about to start in a place that was eerily similar to those from plot lines in spaghetti westerns. It was a policing detachment of nine members protecting an area of seventeen thousand square kilometres, with one road leading in and out. Being a rookie, you want to make sure you've served your time out in the field to garner experiences that will help your future career. You know you are being sent somewhere special when the wardrobe includes northern kit, equipped with huge fur-lined mittens and an extra large parka, and government housing at eighty-eight dollars a month for rent. It has to be a special place if the daily rent is the equivalent to the cost of a daily large double-double and a donut at Timmies.

One of the first memories from my posting was being shown my home: a single, wide trailer with a faulty lock on the front door. In the cold, the pipes would whine and groan under the extreme winter conditions. At least with the multiple heaters roaring and the smell of fresh Swedish decor (IKEA), it became a cosy space for one. I don't think you could fit more than one and a half people in that space.

As days became weeks and weeks became months, I grew to have an affinity for the local people in Fisher Branch. It started almost by mistake, when I arrested an individual from Koostatak First Nations. After I managed to cuff and calmly escort the intoxicated individual into the back of my cruiser, the first thing he asked me, once he got comfortable, was where I was from. My simple response was, "I'm Indian, but not your kind."

He replied, "Who cares, as long as you're Indian."

Another time, a gentleman from Jackhead First Nations wanted to know what reserve I was from. I said, "Punjab First Nations." He asked me if it was near Shamattawa, I casually said, "It's a few thousand miles away." He responded with, "Doesn't matter, its close enough." It's the gems like these that define the kind-hearted people of the harsh North, and allow you to become part of their community.

There is a misconception that people of the reserves are a rowdy and lawless bunch, but I'm one that will forever defend against this statement. Being under the star-filled sky of the wild country, many think that the sidearm is a companion that rarely gets holstered. What I'm here to tell you is, having the gift of the gab is sometimes more important than brawn or might. Sure, I got into a bunch of scrapes that produced minor cuts and bruises, but you chalk that up as experience and one-upmanship amongst friends and colleagues. But at the end of the day, this posting wasn't about bragging rights, it was about something much deeper. It was about connecting with people of the land. For example, I once arrived at a house and gave a Father a subpoena for his son, meaning that his son was being summoned to court to face charges. Finding out that you or a family member is being charged with a crime can often invoke hostility. As I was leaving the residence, the Father noticed my tire was getting low and the next thing I knew he was out in the minus forty degree weather changing the tire on my police car.

One of my most memorable stories happened during the summer of 1999. During this specific day, I was scheduled to work from 3:00 PM to 3:00 AM with my partner Mike. We also had a summer student join us for a few hours at the beginning of shift so that she could get some experience on the road. Fisher Branch, like most limited duration posts, is seldom short of work and the file load depends directly on your ability to keep up. Mike and I decided we weren't going to be hitting the road until we got caught up on investigations. No sooner had we pulled out a stack of files, when my desk phone suddenly began ringing. As I grudgingly picked up the phone a concerned voice started talking at the other end. As the male continued to speak, I started to piece together that his uncle hadn't answered his phone in a couple of days and that he was concerned. My immediate reaction was to tell the caller to call the telephone company to ensure the line was actually working, and have relatives check on the Uncle, considering there were a number of them living in the area. My suggestion didn't impress the caller, so I quickly jotted down his number and took some basic information about the exact location of his uncle's home.

After I hung up the phone, I reached out to Ken, a band constable in the area of the Uncle's residence. Band constables lived in the First Nation communities we policed, and Ken volunteered his time by assisting us in various capacities. On this occasion, he was going to help me find the caller's Uncle. I relayed the information I received from the caller to Ken, and I decided to drive up to the residence with the summer student. The drive from the detachment to the location of the residence was approximately fifty-five kilometres on a windy road, and on an average it took thirty to thirty-five minutes. Here's a little fact for the readers: there are no street names in Peguis, Fisher River or Jackhead. We usually found our way around the reserves using landmarks such as trees, rivers, and broken down cars. The first lesson in policing in northern Canada is to know your area, and it takes a lot of driving to gain operational familiarity, especially in a place like Fisher Branch where your detachment area is about seventeen thousand square kilometres.

As I prepared my duty bag for the road, Ken's static-y voice came over the police radio informing me that he had walked into the Uncle's house and found him on the kitchen floor in a pool of blood, with several pieces of furniture turned upside down. Mike and I looked at each other knowing that a number of protocols needed to be executed immediately. As I instructed Ken to seal off the scene of the crime, Mike and I grabbed our duty bags and jumped into separate police cars and were off with lights and sirens ablaze.

We were racing to the crime scene with dust kicking from our high-speed vehicles. Every once in a while I would glance at the rear-view mirror just to make sure that Mike's fireball was still behind me in the trail of dust. Soon I flew over a bridge, through winding roads, until I approached the town of Hodgson. I looked back in my rear-view mirror again hoping that I hadn't lost Mike. I noticed the spinning fireball that was on my tail was no longer following me, so I decided to call him on the radio to check his location. By this time, I had already blown through Hodgson and was getting worried about his non-response to my several attempts. Something just didn't feel right, since we departed the detachment at the same time, so I hit the brakes hard and spun the cruiser to head back towards Hodgson.

As my police cruiser hurdled back through Hodgson, I approached the windy road and bridge that I had earlier passed. Once I was metres from the bridge, a horrifying image began to materialize in front of me. Mike's heavily damaged police vehicle was lying on a creek bank facing the opposite side of the road. His car had careened off the road and became airborne and landed on the other side of the banks of the creek. As I approached him, I saw that he had already been taken out of his vehicle by bystanders. There were several people by his side that were trying to comfort him. Mike was lucky to have walked away from the wreckage. I quickly checked up on him, secured his duty belt, called for backup, as we now had a homicide and serious motor vehicle accident involving a police car and an injured officer to deal with.

My detachment commander showed up at the scene within a few minutes of the call and was able to take care of the motor vehicle and the slightly banged-up Mike. After a few words with Mike and wishing him a quick recovery, the summer student and I jumped back into the cruiser and roared off north to Fisher River.

Upon arriving at the Uncle's residence, I had a grim feeling in the pit of my stomach that it was going to be a scene I wouldn't soon forget. I asked the summer student to remain in the car while I secured the area. As I slowly walked to the main entrance of the house, the deafening silence was only broken by the groaning of the floor boards. Everything appeared normal at the front entrance, so I approached the door to the living room. As the door creaked open, I could see tons of broken glass all across the hallway and stairs through the dim afternoon sunlight. Ken followed behind me and guided me into the kitchen and family room area where the body lay. As I stepped up to the main floor and looked in the direction of where the body was, I saw a pool of blood that was vast and thick. It appeared to be a scene right out of a horror movie. Even though I would have loved to bet that the individual was deceased, I still had to check for a pulse, as per regulations. As I couldn't get close enough to the body, because it lay in the middle of the pool of blood, I had to be creative and balance on some broken pieces of furniture that were strewn around. With Ken holding on to my one hand and me balanced on some pieces of wood, I was finally able to lean close enough to confirm the absence of a pulse. The body was visibly bruised and deformed due to a number of fractured bones. It appeared that the body had been there for a day or two.

At the direction of the senior constable, who arrived and took charge of the homicide investigation, Ken and I were assigned to the crime scene until the Major Crime section from Winnipeg could arrive. Seeing how they had a homicide to deal with, Ken and I held that scene for over twenty-four hours. It was a long shift, but the company of Ken and the people from the community who brought us bannock, sandwiches, coffee, and water made it memorable. That and the bathroom breaks in the ditch behind the police car.

In the end Mike recovered, the car didn't. Mike had minor cuts and bruises that healed. I don't think there is anything that can stop Mike, as he continues to shine as a true Mountie. My living space eventually got upgraded to a place that had more reliable plumbing and enough space to invite people to come and visit.

Canada is a place teeming with colours, cultures, and mesmerizing experiences. My experience in Fisher Branch went beyond learning policing 101: there I learnt to connect with people who thrive on association and relationships. I thank the people of Peguis, Koostatak, and Jackhead for their love and acceptance of the little, Indian constable posted to their fantastic community. It really was an experience of a lifetime.

PART II

NOWHERE NEAR ORDINARY

DRUMHELLER DAZE
Inspector Ted Smith (Ret.)
Victoria, British Columbia

Finally it was time for our troop's staffing interviews, where I'd be able to discuss where I would be making my start in the RCMP. I entered room A320 in the historic A Block at the RCMP Training Academy—Depot. It was sweltering hot: in 1975 there was no air conditioning and the red-brick building acted as an oven that was baking the stench from the dumpsters behind the mess (the cafeteria). With my eyes watering a little, my staffing interview went like this:

"Ontario, including Ottawa is out of the question," my interviewer stated.

"Um, okay. How about Manitoba, Saskatchewan, or British Columbia?" I asked.

"You'll like Alberta," was his answer.

"Um, okay. A medium to large detachment please," I said.

"Drumheller. Four-man detachment, you'll be number four."

"Thanks," I said dryly.

"Happy to be of service," he said as he pointed to the door.

And just like that I was off to Drumheller, Alberta: a detachment area having six thousand people and policed by four Mounties. What I didn't know then, now that I am stepping into retirement, is how brightly my first weeks in Drumheller would remain in my memory.

As one of the married codgers in the troop, I was able to take a house-hunting trip from Regina. Driving west, as night fell in the Badlands of Alberta, ordered lights beckoned, so closely spaced that I thought I was coming upon a large city. Drumheller may not be so small after all, I thought. But only in the light of day did I discover that by range and section, I had been tricked by the topography into thinking that these were street lights. In fact, they were farmer's yard lights often miles apart.

Descending down into the "ditch," as it was called, my wife and I stayed in the only accommodations in sight, the Alexander Hotel. I would return later, shortly after starting work, to the very same room for a drug overdose case, in fact in the very same bed—sort of a twisted second honeymoon.

Reviewing a vast array of properties, and encouraged by a lifetime of debt opportunities, I laid out fifteen thousand in hard-scrabbled and borrowed cash for a 1927, non-insulated, drooping roof, unpainted, fifteen-amp supplied, dirt-floor basement, six hundred square foot house. The big plus was a commute of thirty yards to the office (less than a minute in heavy traffic). Our realtor and the house seller turned out to be memorable folks, as I had the pleasure of jailing them both for cocaine offences, but that was to be months down the road.

I graduated Depot, got to the detachment, and met my co-workers. My family was making the move in six weeks from Sudbury, Ontario to Drumheller. So, while I was awaiting their arrival, I got to know some of our "regulars" in the Drumheller detachment area. They too were a memorable bunch overall, but a couple of them stand out.

The Mortimer family's eldest daughter was Nola Gay. I first met her while she was on the Bank of Montreal steps howling at the moon like Li'l Abner's dog: more on this family later.

"Frenchie" had been a ranch hand at the James' bunkhouse. He'd come home drunk and thought (apparently) that it would be a good idea to fry up a skillet full of bacon drippings for some supper. Actually, it proved not to be a good idea after all, and the bunkhouse was burnt so flat that I spent the next day with a garden rake looking for any human remains—Frenchie's. I found a band of shiny metal with a couple of bones. My human anatomy classes told me radius and ulna (forearm) and my youth inspired by endless TV advertisements told me Timex, takes a licking and, well you know. It was Frenchie's signature timepiece and in the pre-DNA years, that was proof positive. Unfortunate.

Once, my trainer and I were assigned a next of kin notification (NOK) to do in Wayne, a real Alberta ghost town just down the road from Drumheller. A NOK is when a police officer is tasked to officially notify family that someone has died, or something otherwise bad has happened to a family member. As I drove, I rehearsed the notification, knowing that a poor opening line is, "I'm afraid I have bad news for you."

Wayne is pretty small and I reckoned on finding someone to guide us to the Anderson's residence. I pulled up beside a young woman pushing a loaded baby carriage down the gravel road. I said "Hello, could you tell me where I could find Mrs. Anderson's house?"

"I'm Mrs. Anderson, why?" she answered.

I couldn't stop myself from blurting it out. I could feel it coming out but couldn't stop it: "I'm afraid I have bad news for you." Crap.

"My husband is dead!" she exclaimed.

"No. no, ma'am. It's okay." I corrected her, "It's your father..."

My trainer ended up driving the police car down the road to catch Mrs. Anderson while I pushed the carriage to her home. Not my finest or my most compassionate moment.

Soon after that, our worldly possessions and household effects arrived in Drumheller. The driver, as was apparently the custom, looked for locals to assist him in unloading and unpacking. These young men were great. Grabbing two and four cubic-foot boxes, they ran into the house and ran back for more. The house was pretty small, so in short order the boxes started to stack up on the back porch. About this time my trainer and sergeant arrived to check in on me—the new kid. All of a sudden our helpers literally disappeared, running for their lives back downtown. How was the driver supposed to know that anyone on the street in the daytime in Drumheller was going to be a penitentiary day-parolee? And that the arrival of two uniformed Mounties would scatter his help?

Remember Nola? I met her younger sister Kathy while attending a complaint call of a woman screaming in Starmine. I found her running hysterically from the ramshackle residence of a notorious child molester with her clothes in disarray, crying out "The baby's coming, the baby's coming!" My first reaction had been to get her in the car and hightail it to the hospital for a sexual assault examination. But what did she say? The baby's coming? Oh no! An emergency childbirth!

My second reaction was to recollect my first aid training. Did I have anything sterile, and could I get a shoelace? So, code three (lights and sirens), we went through the slippery centre of town to the ER where we were greeted by Doctor Miller who settled Kathy down right away. He asked her "So, how's little Timmy? He must be a year old by now."

And she replied, "Fine Doctor Miller, Welfare is letting the baby come tomorrow for a visit, *the baby's coming*."

Scotty was a highway patrol chum of mine. He went out into the boonies frequently and made numerous friends, many of whom were first or second generation Danish farmers. We wanted to finish the basement rec-room in the detachment with barn boards, so Scotty researched some and found an abandoned, wooden granary which farmer Skjelnose said we could have for the removal. I was the new recruit and would volunteer for anything.

I was given the directions: southeast quarter section 28, Township 52, Range Road 20, west of the 2nd meridian.

Got it.

We spent the better part of a day disassembling, loading, hauling, moving the boards into the basement, and starting the renovation.

Between the last few boards and the first few refreshments, Tony, our revered secretary, came downstairs and asked no one in particular, "Where did you guys get the wood?"

"At old man Skjelnose's back quarter. Why?" we answered.

"'Cause old man Solvison just called and said some punks stole his granary from south-*west* quarter section 28, Township 52, Range Road 20, west of the 2nd meridian."

It was months before we discharged our penance to Mr. Solvison, but I sure learned my Alberta township grid system.

And while we're on the subject of renovating the basement rec-room.... the White House Hotel, across the street from the Alexander, had burnt to the ground that winter. I guess misfortune is a relative thing though, as the local regulars (theirs and ours) no longer had a place "where everyone knew their name". For us, it was easier for a few weeks to find some of our wanted people as the residents of that hole-in-the-wall looked for new lodging.

Another piece of good fortune was that the White House owner had an underground cold room where he kept his stock: Uncle Ben's Beer, pickled eggs, and kielbasa.

In return for the good deed of helping him (when off duty) cleanout his cold storage of water-damaged, yet still palatable, jarred goods, we were awarded permanent custody of said goods. Downstairs in the wood paneled sanctuary after work, one dollar yielded an unlabelled beer, an egg, and four inches of sulphur-infused sausage. We ate like kings. The resulting perfumed atmosphere, however, ensured that Sophie, our cleaner, didn't venture downstairs for nearly a month.

In the beginning, I felt like Ben Johnson—juiced, pumped, and ready to go and loving it right out of the gate! That's the way a first detachment is supposed to be, a cradle in which you learn how to be a responsible adult and yet still see every detail from a student's point of view. Everything was new, everything was exciting. If I could leave one message for new Mounties, it would be to jump into your first detachment with both feet. It will be the best experience of your working life.

ON A BOAT GOING NOWHERE
Tammy Marshall, Civilian Member
Nanaimo, British Columbia

Every 2010 Olympic and Paralympic experience is unique and personal. For me, being born in Vancouver and growing up in the suburbs made going home for the Olympics and Paralympics extra special. The Games were very exciting: the athletes, sports, competition, and medals; the pavilions and international "houses"; the camaraderie, crowds, and celebrations; tourism, nationalism, and multiculturalism; and of course, the indescribable feeling of being a part of one of the biggest international sporting events.

As an RCMP law enforcement support telecommunication operator (LESTO) in Nanaimo, British Columbia, I had already attended several training exercises in preparation for the Winter Olympics. However, nothing could prepare me for the unique experience of living on a large boat going nowhere.

Despite the lengthy LESTO title, my job is more commonly known as a police telecommunication operator, often referred to as an operator or dispatcher. My duties include answering emergency and non-emergency calls for service, and dispatching the files that are created to the police officers on duty. I am a sworn civilian member of the RCMP, sworn auxiliary constable, and I am completing my master's of arts in professional communication in 2011. It is through my university studies that I chose to write this story, drawn to symbolic interaction theory and concepts of place, home, and material culture.

During the 2010 Winter Olympic Games, approximately six thousand integrated security employees were given accommodation on three cruise ships docked in the Vancouver, British Columbia harbour. As a police dispatcher, I was one of the "security workforce" personnel who, for thirty-two nights, resided on one of the vessels. Fascinated by this encounter, I began to examine the boat as a home, observing how people interacted with each other, and related to the ships as meaningful temporary residences. These experiences, relationships, and interactions are at the heart of my Olympic story, and are chronologically reshaped from my journal excerpts, which I share with you in hopes of offering a different perspective on the Games.

It is January 19, 2010, and we are learning about the Carnival's *Elation*. That's the name of the cruise ship that we will be staying on: approximately seventy dispatchers from all over British Columbia, in addition to almost six thousand other law enforcement employees of various rank and classification will be on this and two other ships.

We begin with two days of venue tours in Richmond, Vancouver, and Whistler, guided by RCMP Staff Sergeant Margaret Shorter and Sergeant Pepin Wong. What a nice surprise to have Marg as our tour guide, as she and I first met in 2008 at the International Association of Women Police Conference in Darwin, Australia. During the tours, our supervisor gives us word from the Integrated Security Unit (ISU) that we are double-booked in rooms on the ship, although they are unable to tell us who we'll be rooming with. People are disappointed to have to share, however, at some point most were forewarned of this likelihood. We are assured our roommates will be from our own section (dispatch), but it's unknown if they will follow the same shift schedule.

January 22 marks the first day of work at the ISU Operational Communications Centre (OCC) for the 2010 Olympics and Paralympics. Located in Richmond, the ISU OCC is ready to go, complete with three enormous television screens so we can watch the Games and the news while we work.

Once we embark on the boat, we are not allowed to change roommates because everything is computerized and tracked by "mobilization". The cruise ship identification card we've all been issued allows us on and off the boat and is also a key to our room. It is associated to our credit card, so exchanging keys with others is forbidden. These are among the things the staff relations representatives (SRRs) tell us, noting also that no one is allowed to take food off the boat due to federal customs regulations. Meanwhile, dispatchers are asking questions from members already staying on the ship to find out other things about laundry and spa facilities, food quality, noise in the hallways, gym hours and equipment, pools and hot tubs, and, can you really get a bucket of four beers for five bucks?

Venues continue to do their "sweeps" on January 24 and 25, the thorough checks of venues by the Tactical Troops to ensure they are safe and secure. The police officers begin to sign on with dispatch, but the night is slow and only seven of us are working. The SRRs send an email stating that employees who are already on a different ship (Holland America's *Statendam*) in the Vancouver harbour are divided: fifty per cent say they think it is best to room with someone who follows the same schedule, while the other half prefers different schedules. We also hear from some police officers that most are enjoying their stay on the boat so far.

With only a few days before check in, I am learning more about the ship we will be staying on. The three hundred million dollar *Elation* is one of Carnival Cruise Lines many vessels and has a maximum capacity of 2,634, including nine hundred and twenty crew members on regular cruises to Mexico and California. The *Elation* has a number of sister ships with similarly provocative names, like *Fantasy, Ecstasy, Sensation, Fascination, Imagination, Inspiration,* and *Paradise*. Carnival's website provides a comprehensive description of the *Elation* including most of the facilities, so we know what to expect: dining options, atriums, panorama elevators, bars, lounges, gym, sports deck, sun deck, beauty salon, spa, and running track. This will all be available to us like a regular cruise, although the shopping mall, casino, library, piano bar, and fancy dining room are not in service for this particular journey without a voyage. Today, I am literally waiting for my ship to come in.

It is now January 28, and with all the hype, the good ship *Elation* has grown into such an intriguing, unknown entity. People are anxious, as if getting ready to meet a blind date. The *Elation* is almost human—superhuman—and we aren't even on it yet. It docked this morning and a security sweep was to be completed by noon. The first word from those who checked in is that the rooms are very small, two beds "toe-to-toe" in each, and that it's quite a hike through the terminal and pier to actually get on the boat. One person called it a "funhouse", brightly decorated in orange and teal, both inside and outside the staterooms. One of the dispatchers checked in to find only a single bed, disappointed at the claustrophobic feeling of an inside room, but ever-so-glad to have a room to herself. Another dispatcher claims that napping was difficult this afternoon due to the noise of people checking in and getting settled. Meanwhile, we have discovered that the *Elation* was recently home to the world's first International Cougar Cruise from San Diego, California to Ensenada, Mexico. Oh my!

It is January 29, check in day for me, and as we anticipate our accommodations for the next month, I say in jest, "We are all in the same boat." This joke becomes trite as time goes on. Most people haven't slept much during the relocation from hotel to boat and some are transitioning between their shifts. Meanwhile, the whole mystery roommate issue is getting to people as well. Some are disappointed when they find out who their roommate is while others are happy—a sigh of relief. Some find themselves the first to move in, with further occupancy expected, yet unknown. Others open the stateroom door to find the belongings of a stranger, but the stranger is not present. There is such an unknown: an empty bed, a room full of belongings of an unknown person, an acquaintance to-be, a potential new friend.

Some people are on the pier side facing the container terminal, while others are on the inside and have no window, others face the ocean and mountains, complete with a decent view of North Vancouver. One dispatcher says she can hear the continuous beeping of forklifts backing up during the night. She says the dispatchers' rooms are all near each other and that we are lucky to be near the laundry room.

People are all abuzz about *being on the boat, at the boat, when I get to the boat, the shuttle to the boat, the spa on the boat*. In addition, there is talk of the boat gym, the boat bar, the running deck on the boat, and so on. Lance Armstrong might say *it's not about the boat*. I say it is. At 5PM, a taxi drops off my colleague and me at the cruise ship terminal and we get our cruise card. We must drape it onto the other accreditation passes we received on the first day, to be worn at all times on the ship. We receive our luggage tags and shuffle our baggage off to the handlers who will get it to our room. The procedure is virtually the same as when you board a cruise ship for a real cruise.

We walk through a wireless Internet room full of computers set-up especially for us in the terminal, available 24/7, and then make our way down a long hallway, some stairs, and down an outdoor walkway to the boat. It is fortuitous that the regular cruise ship services have been adjusted to suit our schedules because typically, as shift workers, it is we who have become accustomed to adjusting our schedules based on access to services.

Security scans my card and takes a photo, the standard procedure upon boarding the vessel for the first time. From here on in, everyone must scan their cards as they embark and disembark the ship. We go directly to our rooms, and we transition from uncertainty into certainty about the reality of sharing a room and with whom. I slide my card into the key slot, open the door, and see someone else's luggage and clothes, half unpacked on her bed. Realizing my roommate is not in the room, I notice her name on her luggage tag. We have never met. Other colleagues tell me she is very nice and that we will get along well.

I read the standard welcome greeting in the room and some basic instructions. It is late into the night when I finish doing laundry, unpacking, and personalizing my part of the room. With two closets and some drawers, it really isn't difficult to fit all my stuff into compartments, leaving half for my roommate. The living space is small—two single beds—hers by the window and mine by the wall, which I like. Already, I find this whole idea of residing on a large boat going nowhere very fascinating.

The boat is indeed orange and teal all over and it's pretty safe to say the decor is nothing short of tacky. It looks like a late 1980s style, although this ship was built in the nineties. All purchases are in American funds, so the guest services desk doles out a steady stream of American quarters for laundry. I am in awe and I am contemplative. I can't help think this cruise ship convergence feels like everyone is gathering for an occasion like a wedding, funeral, convocation, or reunion. Indeed, we are here for a celebration—the 2010 Olympic Winter Games—but in the end, the reality is we are here to work. Some people are disappointed with these accommodations, but this experience is so unusual that I can't help but feel intrigued.

Typically, I prefer exploration and freedom over manufactured experiences, however, in times like this, when work is at a maximum and free time at a minimum, there is something wonderfully convenient about this one-stop-shop that we have here. And really, how can I complain when someone is regularly picking up my dishes from outside my door, making my bed, and cleaning my room? I allow my senses to go into holiday mode with all the music, buffets, drinks, and amenities at my fingertips, and even activities in which to partake.

I am writing this entry in the restaurant of the tenth floor Lido deck, open round-the-clock for the duration of this adventure, complete with its plastic peacock feather design. The Spanish music is creating a sense of somewhere else—a vacation—and it is intertwined with Patsy Cline favourites (also sung by a male with a Spanish accent), and encored by "Que Sera Sera". The next set starts off with Willie Nelson's "You Were Always on my Mind" which may have prompted a tear on better days, but amongst the tacky decor, I am pensive, but far from somber. Besides, I am certain the Gypsy Kings will return shortly. In the background, the vacuum suction sounds are overpowering. It's 2:00 AM and the cleaning crew is doing their work. One of the staff tells me this is her first "docked cruise" and that translates to forty-two days in port for her with very little time off.

It's January 30, and I am thinking about how anyone can create an image or identity to portray while on a cruise or vacation. On this ship, however, everyone knows someone, if not many people, so the idea of fabricating identities isn't really an option. Despite being on an "accommodation vessel", the atmosphere is very similar to a real cruise, simulated so well that I tend to forget I'm not on holiday. Going to and from work is the reminder. It's funny how we pay big money for grandiose vacations to foreign lands, yet a replica cruise experience can indeed be successfully created without ever leaving the Vancouver harbour. That might explain why I've started referring to this experience as "this trip" and why others are starting to call the boat "home". I have also heard it referred as "the hotel" or "the office".

It's January 31, and the final wave of dispatchers arrive today, including two gals from home (Nanaimo OCC) who lucked out when they got paired up in a swanky deluxe stateroom complete with a fridge, two leather couches, a balcony with ocean view, bar, and bathtub with jets.

There are now three ships in the harbour, docked until March 2, after the Olympics are over and before the Paralympics begin. Holland America's *Statendam* arrived first, the Carnival's *Elation* arrived January 28, and Holland America's *Oosterdam* arrived today. A friend recently questioned whether I was worried about the security risk of the three ships in the harbour, commenting that they are like "sitting ducks" as far as terrorist threats go. I'm not sure why I'm not terribly concerned, and I'm satisfied with our security crews, including the marine section constantly patrolling the water.

In a completely unrelated thought, there are small pockets of time and space in which to use the Internet; the ten-minute walk from the boat to the terminal can be a bit chilly when it's cold outside. Instead, in the name of time and convenience, I often opt to fork out the twenty-five cents US, per minute for a somewhat reliable Internet connection on my laptop in my room. Speaking of rooms, with the stewards catering to shift workers, we each get a choice of four blocks of time in which to have our rooms cleaned. We simply leave the coloured piece of plastic with the preferred time block on our outer-door handles, much like a Do Not Disturb sign, and the stewards come clean our rooms at the selected times. This is a ship, not a hardship.

Every night at 6:00 PM, the ship's activity announcements are broadcast throughout the boat. "Karaoke with Salminella in the Cole Porter Lounge," the man's voice announces. Midnight meet-and-greets are also common, and for a list of all activities, one need not look further than the weekly itinerary of activities that we receive under our doors much like when on a real cruise. Tonight, my co-worker and I opted for a glass of wine after our shift.

It was 4:00 AM and strange to see people coming in for their breakfasts and morning coffee, the latter of which could be compared to sludge. As for the buffet-style dining, I find it is all starting to taste the same, and it seems like only breakfast food is available when I'm there. Perhaps that's better than waking up to prawns or ham, or the pizza or sandwiches that are always available. If you're really lucky, though, you might be awake when the stir-fry bar is available.

One of the dining staff told me there are approximately six hundred employees from forty-one countries working on the ship, two people to a room on the lower decks (ours are mid), and most employees working nine to ten hour days, every day, and no days off. Their shifts are staggered and they do get a chance to go see the town at some point, taking the same shuttle as we do from the ship to Waterfront Station downtown.

Every day I expect to meet my roommate but February 2 to 6 goes by and still our paths haven't crossed, even at shift change. She left me a note on her days off, saying she'd be away visiting family, so who knows how long it will be until we meet. In the meantime, I'm feeling a bit at odds with the ship. I paid forty American dollars for a slow—and short—wireless connection in my room. I really wanted to do my homework in my pyjamas while sipping espresso brewed with my French press and travel kettle, the latter of which has since gone missing, along with my candles. Turns out housekeeping confiscated them while cleaning my room, and left me a note about the "hazardous items" found in my room. I understand the candles, but the kettle, really? The staff also left my television blaring all night while people were sleeping next door. Today, this ship has made me frustrated.

I went to the dress rehearsal for Olympic opening ceremonies today at BC Place Stadium with approximately thirty thousand other people. My cousin's girlfriend was among the ceremony participants and all volunteers received a few tickets for friends and family. The whole production was wonderful and not only did I feel proud to be Canadian, but I also felt proud to be from Vancouver.

It is a big day, February 8, and not just because of this amazing ceremony. Today I finally met my roommate! We were in the room at the same time, and it turns out we do get along very well. Meanwhile, we have learned that one of the other ships doesn't have laundry facilities, so that's why people bring their bottles of booze, plates of cheese, and miscellaneous party snacks to our laundry room, laying them all out on the ironing tables while they drink, chat, and party. The laundry room has become quite a hangout actually: a space, a gathering place, a bistro, a lounge, and, rumour has it, a haven for romantic getaways.

There is nothing like running on the top deck of a stationary cruise ship at midnight in early February. Absolutely divine! I ran in both directions so I could enjoy both views of Vancouver at night, including Vancouver harbour and Grouse Mountain, shining like a beacon in the background. All alone and fully present in the moment, I ran around and around as raindrops delicately fell on my face and lightly matted my hair. This is my new favourite ship activity. While I was running, I recalled the day the bus didn't pick us up after work and we ended up getting a ride back to the cruise ship terminal with some members who drove us in two vans. It made me realize the bus culture is an interesting thing in itself. According to one driver, up to ninety buses were hired to transport staff to and from the ships, venues, and various work locations. Every bus ride is different although it's typically the same group of us transported together each day, members and dispatchers working shifts much like "watches" back home.

February 12 marks the official opening ceremonies for the 2010 Winter Olympic Games. It was so surreal to watch it unfold on TV as we worked! The host city is making a good impression so far, continuing to make me feel proud to be from Vancouver. Had there not been a tragic and fatal luge accident, these Games would have begun on a perfect note. This past weekend, I flew home on the floatplane from downtown Vancouver to downtown Nanaimo. I passed a co-worker in transit as she was heading back to Vancouver after indulging in a similar getaway. Flying time was fifteen minutes each way and it was rather turbulent but fun. The pilot invited me to sit in the cockpit, and I enjoyed staring at sunshine and landing on the water.

Upon my return, I walked back to the ship through the east end, Vancouver's well-known drug-ridden area of homelessness. When I got back to the pier, security staff wouldn't let me walk to the ship because the truck drivers had complained that pedestrian traffic was dangerous, and now people are banned from walking to and from the ship terminal and Heatley Overpass. One must take a shuttle, taxi, or vehicle in and out of the area which means the shuttle now runs 24/7, although not as regularly after midnight. The terminal security vehicle brought me in and I did some homework before I jumped ship to check out the *Oosterdam*, the best of the three ships, in my opinion. The atmosphere was comfortable and the dining room offered fresh food, cooked to order. I had steak and scallops and fresh pasta. Bars (non-alcoholic) seem to be the thing here: salad, pasta and pizza, juice, fruit, dessert, and a wonderful entree bar. Oh my, what a discovery!

Yesterday was a tired day for many. The big news of February 15 was the discovery of more and more people going to the *Oosterdam* for meals and to the gym. Likewise, some of the *Oosterdam* residents are coming to our boat, forming a bit of an "us and them" division. They bring their laundry and alcohol to the *Elation* and party all night in the laundry room, propping the door open with a crushed beer can to avoid excessive heat from the dryers. It is always occupied and it's difficult to find a time to do laundry. This causes people to opt for the eighteen American dollars, per laundry bag that the ship will wash and dry for you, returning it to your room within two days, folded or on hangers.

I went to an Olympic hockey game today, February 17, with a gal from work. Finland beat Belarus five to one at Canada Hockey Place, also known as GM Place. On our way to the game, we went to the *Oosterdam* and had made while-you-wait omelettes with fresh-squeezed orange juice. It's funny how everyone is falling in love with "the Ooster", its new nickname. Some people just go there and hang out by the pool. I hear the running track is mid-ship and five hundred metres around, making it easy to tally your distance, however, our boat's running track is on the top deck so you have wide open sky above you, making the *Elation*'s more appealing to me. It seems like a better option than the gym, where people are running on treadmills going nowhere, on a boat going nowhere. Tonight we found out that one of the engine room employees of the *Statendam* has a form of leprosy called Hansen's disease. Yikes!

Off to the *Oosterdam* I went last night to see the movie *Funny People* in the cozy theatre with leather recliners. I couldn't help but go up and have dessert before going back to the *Elation* where I ran into some of the other dispatchers. You really can't go anywhere on the boats without running into someone you know. Some people like this inevitability while others prefer privacy.

It's February 20, and on my way back from downtown there were so many people waiting for the shuttle: security workforce employees and ship staff. It's a good thing two shuttles came at the same time. When we arrived at the ship terminal building, we went through the usual routine. The security workforce personnel stick to the right and pass by, showing accreditation passes, while the ship employees go left and through a security screening area similar to those found in airports. It seems odd because we are all as one on the shuttle, then we are segregated in order to board the ship.

It's now February 21, and I've been reflecting on the huge amount of trust that goes into the police officer security members at the terminal gates. They are always busy screening incoming vehicles, shuttles and buses, and using some sort of metal device to check them all, as well as checking the accreditations of people entering the terminal. In addition to the airport-style security for ship staff inside the terminal, we also must trust that luggage is free of dangerous items, and that the food won't make us sick, especially for those like me who go from ship-to-ship experimenting with different food. Speaking of which, during dinner on the *Oosterdam* on February 22, the Ooster staff announced there would be special RCMP dinners Wednesday through Friday, business-casual attire required. The manager gave permission for us to attend even though we are staying on a different ship.

It's February 24, and people are already starting to receive check-out instructions. That brings sadness for some, realizing how they've come to appreciate the unique boat experience, although many originally thought they were going to hate it. Some say they can't figure out why, on one hand they are looking forward to getting off the boat, but on the other they know they will soon miss it. Others can't wait to disembark; they just want to go home, or anywhere other than the ship. Some even vow to never take a cruise, as if somehow traumatized by this experience. While a co-worker, my roommate, and I stayed up and chatted over wine, some colleagues sang karaoke in the ship's lounge and danced at the disco, the nightclub adorned by creepy red and white plastic jesters. There had been talk of maybe playing hide-and-seek, which would be fun with a large group on a cruise ship, but it didn't materialize. What is not fun is that, due to the noise factor, some people are seeking alternate places to sleep: the library, theatre benches, closed bar and lounges, hallway, and ship terminals where the computers are.

The women's gold medal game took place yesterday, February 25, and I met some of my friends and former hockey teammates at Canada's Molson Hockey House to watch it. The venue is basically a big building full of people and big screens, as well as a stage where the band The Odds played a few songs during the game intermissions. It was awesome to be amongst so many women watching the game, many of us hockey players ourselves. How great it was to see Canada beat the US two to zero here in Vancouver. Nothing is sweeter than Olympic GOLD!

On my way back to the ship, I attended the Aboriginal pavilion's traditional singing and dancing, as well as the popular nine-minute video presentation titled *We Are Here*. As for today, I went to the spa on our boat and got a wonderful massage before hitting up the steam room. Then I headed to the *Oosterdam* for the special RCMP appreciation dinner. It was just like formal sit-down dining on a *real cruise*, and the servers brought our menus, food, and drinks to the table. This meal was fantastic, and we all ate a lot, including dessert. When I got back to my room, even though I should have gone to sleep, I took advantage of the last opportunity to chat with my roommate over a glass (or two) of wine.

Fast forward to March 3, and I've resigned to the fact that my ship has sailed. It is no longer a home, as I and seventeen other dispatchers relocate to the Hyatt Hotel in downtown Vancouver for the Paralympics. All three ships were scheduled to leave the Vancouver harbour yesterday, and they are becoming a distant memory. I know I will miss the boat, but I am happy to regain my privacy and anonymity. Although I'll treasure all the special moments and people, I won't miss that sometimes smothering feeling of forced experiences and running into familiar people everywhere I go. Still, I can't help reflect with thanks on thirty-two nights of living on a cruise ship while working at the 2010 Winter Olympics. It was truly a unique experience both from a personal and professional standpoint.

Working the 2010 Games was definitely a highlight in my career with the RCMP and I am grateful to have been chosen to assist in such a huge, international endeavour. I heard on the radio that counselling is available for Vancouver Olympic Committee employees who worked for several years towards this big event and who might suffer from post-Olympic depression. I, the dispatcher from Nanaimo, have not experienced any negative or devastating effects, however, I anticipate from time to time that I may have slight pangs of longing for an amazing experience that can never be duplicated. It is a rare opportunity to work the Olympic and Paralympic Games, and an even lesser likelihood to spend over a month living on a boat going nowhere.

THE YELLOW STRIPE
Constable Marilyn Emond, neé Campbell
Halifax, Nova Scotia

(As told by a senior RCMP officer to a junior member)

A simple vertical yellow stripe
Is said, "Must be worn with pride"
For all those who have come before you,
For all those who have died.

You will walk where others fear to tread,
You will protect those in need,
You will stand tall where others tremble,
The fight, you will lead.

To Queen and country you will swear
Your oath, loyal and true
To serve amongst the finest
Canada's family in blue.

Proud to be Canadian
Shoulder to shoulder, thin blue line
Proud to make a difference
One person at a time.

You will comfort a dying victim,
Wipe away a child's tear,
Console a grieving loved one,
Ease a community's fear.

Yes, you will arrest the bad guys,
Get in a scrape or two.
Stand up tall and dust off
That proud yellow stripe on blue.

And if one day that yellow stripe
Should fall horizontal to the ground,
Take heart young Mountie, you're not alone
Your friends, they are around.

Your family in blue will carry you,
They will see justice done.
For you they will stand, as the saying goes
"One for all and all for one."

And if like the sun, that yellow stripe
Should fade when the day is done,
A grieving nation will mourn the loss
Of another daughter or son.

The flag will fly at half-mast.
But we, we will stand tall.
You did your duty, you made us proud;
"Above and beyond the call."

A sea of red will stand in tribute
While the bagpipes play
To honour your life, cut short,
Was lost, at the closing of the day.

But for now, young Mountie,
Stand firm. Stand fast. Stand true.
To protect and serve proudly
With that yellow stripe on blue.

A TYPICAL AUTUMN DAY
Corporal Kristopher Boyle
London, Ontario

It was a typical autumn day in Ontario. The kids were back in school, leaves were changing colours, and Thanksgiving Day was right around the corner. I wish that was the memory that was stored deep in my mind. Sadly, what was about to unfold still tends to keep me up at night. Tragedy has a way of doing that.

In the town where I live there is a campground and a pioneer village. Throughout the year the pioneer village does reenactments, picnics, and other wholesome family activities. Among the list of events, every autumn the village offers up a series of breakfasts during the Thanksgiving weekend. Personally, I find these types of things quaint, yet pointless. My wife and her family, however, thought it would be a great idea to have a get-together and partake. I am not a morning person, but I also knew there would be food—the math seemed to add up.

We went to the Pioneer Village on the morning of October 6, 2007. The family crowded into the "restaurant" where the breakfast was taking place. To my surprise, the food was pretty good, even with the leaky roof and crammed room. Afterwards, we decided to take a walk around the village with the little ones in tow. The leaves had turned their usual breathtaking colours and there was a slight, damp chill. The morning had seen its share of rain, but it was quiet now. As I walked around, I could smell the air and feel the ground under my feet. All-in-all it was a typical family get-together on a typical autumn day.

The ride back to my mother's house was quick and uneventful. The mid-Saturday television schedule left little to be desired, so I flipped the channel to the all-news station. The day's earlier breakfast was starting to settle in and I thought I would hop on the computer instead. Even this activity seemed to be more of a time-filler than productive. At some point between this moment in time and the next thirty minutes my soul and life were rocked and have been a little different ever since.

As I sat staring at the computer monitor, I could hear the news in the background. To this date, I cannot remember the name of the news anchor, but I can recall the words with crystal clarity: "...a young Mountie was gunned down early this morning in the small town of Hay River, Northwest Territories..."

Hold on a second, I thought, Chris Worden works in Hay River. I got up and went to the TV. As I turned into the living room, I could see his face looking back at me on the fifty inch, rear projection screen. It was the picture I remember joking about with him when it was taken five years prior.

Towards the end of RCMP training at Depot in Saskatchewan, cadets are lined up in alphabetical order to have four pictures taken. The first is taken wearing a business shirt so that your warrant card has a face on it— your police ID. The second was an entire troop photo, akin to a class photo. The third picture is a solo shot with the cadet wearing full Red Serge with a Canadian flag in the background. Big smiles were encouraged for the third one. Then came the last picture. Much like the third, the cadets are wearing their Red Serge and hat, however, they are asked to remove the leather cross strap, to this day, I don't know why. This last photo is the official one for your file. I remember that Chris and I laughed and rolled our eyes as they said, "Take the cross strap off of your shoulder, and don't smile. This is the picture they will use if you end up dead on the job." That was the picture that was on the big screen.

Oh shit.

The news story had moved on. Goddamn news. I changed the channel frantically and couldn't find the story anywhere else. It was the top story of the day and they had already moved on to some other piece. I ran back to the computer.

It was September 8, 2001 when I first met Chris Worden. Cadets are flown in from across Canada to attend RCMP training in Saskatchewan. When training is completed, the new members of the RCMP are scattered back across the country, many not ending up where they started. The training lasts about six months and the cadets are placed into a group called a "troop". I didn't know it at the time, but Chris and I were destined to be assigned to the same troop. Both he and I were recruited out of Ontario. It turns out that the RCMP had booked a few of us on the same plane to fly to Depot in Regina.

As I waited for my luggage to arrive down the belt a tall, young, and shaved-bald fellow introduced himself to me.

"Hi, I'm Chris," he said with a smile that I can still see to this day. Over the next few months, and into a Saskatchewan winter, we became not only troop mates but friends. I was with him when he bought his girlfriend Jodie an engagement ring in town and fortunate enough to stand up with him at his wedding a couple of years later in Ingersoll, Ontario.

Chris, a former university football player, was posted from Depot training right to the Northwest Territories. I believe he was onto his third posting before the morning of October the 6th. As it would later be revealed, Chris was called back out between shifts to answer a call for service. This call turned out to be uneventful. On his way back home he saw three people leaving a local drug house. They were about to get into a taxi when Chris approached. It was just after 4:00 AM. During this transaction, one of the men ran off and Chris gave chase.

What Chris didn't realize was that this man was in town to deal drugs, and had been flashing a handgun around for the past few days. The chase only lasted several hundred metres. The suspect was five feet and two inches tall, overweight, and losing the race. He only really had two options: give up or fight.

While running, the suspect reached for his gun and fired three shots that struck Chris. The bullet to the neck is most likely the one that killed Chris almost instantly. He was found several hours later by his co-workers and pronounced dead at the local hospital. The suspect fled but was later caught and is now serving a life sentence. He won't be up for parole until 2034.

October 15, 2007 was the day of Chris' funeral. Jodie had asked that I participate as an honourary pallbearer. The RCMP, in times like these, truly operates as a single, focused family. As Chris' troop mate and friend, every effort was made to make sure I could participate and had someone to talk to if I needed. I never experienced an RCMP reaction like that. It was truly heartwarming. But, frankly, I hope I never see it again.

I stood there, turned out in my Red Serge, Stetson, and boots at the front gates to Parliament Hill. The hearse was to my immediate left. The pipers and mounted unit were up front. One horse had no rider—intentionally symbollic. The moment was surreal. I don't think my boots had ever received that much polish and shine. It turns out there are only some things in this life that we can control and, at that moment, the polish of my boots was in my control.

As the drums and pipers started the march, I remember giving the hearse a gentle pat on the side of the door and thinking, "Let's go buddy, I've got you from here." The slow crawl of the procession wound its way past the parliament buildings and the thousands of people who had turned out to line the streets and pay tribute to Chris. There were young and old, men and women, civilian and service personnel that stood there silently. As Chris would approach and pass by, some children saluted along with the serving men and women. I would be lying if I told you that I didn't cry. I did.

The funeral was a touching tribute to Chris. As his family, friends, and co-workers spoke they described a guy that I knew quite well. I always knew Chris was a good guy, but I didn't really appreciate how consistent he was about it. As his baby girl fussed in the pew, all I could do was sit there and make sure that the polish on my boots hadn't scuffed while trying not to think about my daughter sitting at home, waiting for her dad to come back from Ottawa.

Christopher John Worden was laid to rest at Ottawa's Beachwood Cemetery among other Mounties, both young and old. As the ceremony came to a close, each of Chris' co-workers and troop mates lined up to give a final salute to him. I stepped up and gave the best salute I could muster. I don't think I have ever been so tall and still. Life feels a little different now. As I stood there I could still smell the Canadian autumn air; it was crisp and cool. The difference now was that, as the leaves lay beneath my polished boots; this wasn't a typical autumn day.

Editor's Note: The Foreword of this book was written by Chris Worden's wife, Jodie Worden.

TO THE DOGS
Constable Aaron Sheedy
Toronto, Ontario

In the spring of 2005, the stars aligned and I was selected to become the drug-dog handler for the Toronto Airport Detachment. At two and half years of service, I would be the most junior dog handler in the country. With very little notice and a great deal of apprehension I was off to Alberta to become an RCMP dog handler.

Dog handlers in the RCMP come in basically three varieties. First, there are puppy handlers. These are volunteers who take over the training of a German shepherd puppy from the time that the puppy is ready to leave its mom and the breeding program in Alberta until it is ready to be put into service as a police dog and paired with a general duty dog handler.

The general duty dog handlers, the second type, are the heart and soul of the RCMP police dog service program. With their four-legged partners, they can track down lost children, fleeing criminals, guns or other discarded evidence, and quell hostile individuals with a snarl or bite. My experience with these dogs is that their bite is worse than their bark, and their bark is really scary.

I was once working with Corporal George Voelk, the general duty dog handler in Toronto and his German shepherd, Nash. We were working in an abandoned hotel near Pearson Airport. The scenario was that I was barricaded in one of the rooms and refused to come out. I had the protective sleeve on one arm, and I was yelling through the door provoking George, and by extension, Nash. He sent the dog in and, in a flash of fur and bone-white teeth, I was dragged to the ground and then out of the room. Nash is a small but mighty dog, as she proved by dragging my two hundred and fifty pounds out the door! At one point, she tugged and yanked on my arm and we were eye to eye. She looked me square in the eye and shook her head with my arm in her jaws, and growled as if to say, "I would kill you if I could." Two things became clear: First, don't yell at George when Nash is around, she takes it personally, and second, these dogs are amazing animals with amazing training.

The general duty dog teams are also trained to detect the odour of drugs or explosives. The handlers are exceptionally fit and the dogs are exceptional in every way. The program is rigorous for both the dog and handler, and by the time the team gets to training they have been tested several times. A well-trained RCMP Police Dog Service team (dog and handler) is an awesome policing tool, second to none in the world. Knowing this pedigree, I showed up in Alberta to be issued, and train with, an RCMP narcotics-detector dog.

The narcotic-detector dog team is the third variation of police dog teams in the RCMP. We're not quite as fit as our general duty counterparts and we, with our dogs, only do one thing: search for drugs. So sometimes it is a little less glamorous, and we're often tasked heavily with other duties in our detachments that compete for our drug searching time.

There were four candidates for our course: Constable Trent Sperlie, Constable Greg Hawkins, Constable Craig Webb, and myself. We met our instructor, Sergeant Bob Lowe, a seasoned general duty dog handler turned trainer. Our course was scheduled for two and a half months with Bob, who was retiring the day our course finished. We were his last hurrah.

After two days of settling in, attending classroom lectures, and of course completing RCMP paperwork, we were ready to meet the finely tuned RCMP K-9s that were to be our partners. As we walked past the proud German shepherds to our kennel areas to meet our dogs, Bob explained that it was important for us to understand that these dogs, our drug dogs, come to the RCMP for a reason.

There was a silence as we stood outside the cages looking at our dogs. Levi was a trained black Labrador retriever who was already living with Trent, so they had a head start —it was just Trent who had to do the learning. There was Tank, a slow-lumbering chocolate Labrador retriever who was assigned to Craig. Greg's dog was possibly the most hyperactive dog I had ever seen, a golden retriever named Dodger. And my dog was Nytra, a female black Labrador retriever.

The adjustment period was trying. Trent and Levi were already bonded, and Levi already knew what "the game" was. The game is hide-and-seek, where the dogs sniff out drug odour, sit beside the drugs, and then wait excitedly for their toy. The rest of us had quite a learning curve, dogs and handlers alike, as we worked out the routine that would establish the basis of the dogs' training, and the ability for the dogs to indicate the presence of a drug odour to us, the handlers.

We quickly figured out what Bob meant when he said that these dogs come to us for "a reason". These animals were freakin' insane. Other than the requisite mental disorders, there are other requirements to be an RCMP narcotics-detector dog. Typically the animals are in very good health and are screened medically before even being considered. We use what are affectionately called "floppy-eared" breeds as opposed to the "pointy-eared" general duty dogs. The floppy-eared dogs, such as the retriever breeds, are fairly easily trained, and their natural desire to chase down birds and bring them back can be converted to seeking out drug odour. The dogs are less threatening in appearance, so we can work around the public without people fleeing in fear...most times.

We were slowly getting the hang of handling a drug dog. One of the most important things I learned working with these dogs is that love is a fuel. The closer they are bonded to you, the more legitimate the relationship between handler and dog, the more the dog will do.

We were all working at our own pace and the dogs were hitting training milestones at different times. The goals were different too. Trent and Levi pretty much ran from drug hide to drug hide. Levi would slam his butt down beside the hide and wait for his toy. If that wasn't evident enough he'd bark, just once, to let Trent know that he smelled the drugs. Trent and Levi made the rest of us look like bumbling clowns as we tried to figure out our dogs.

Craig and Tank were a perfect match. They'd stroll from hide to hide and eventually find it, no big excitement. Craig never broke a sweat as his slow moving dog would get there when he got there.

The first time Greg had Dodger out to train, we were in a warehouse at the old Penhold military base near Red Deer. Dodger just stood at the end of leash and barked looking up at the ceiling. He didn't follow direction, the dog didn't even know how to sit on command, let alone find drugs and then sit. There they were, the dog not knowing what to do and Greg not knowing what to do, and Bob yelling at them to go search for the drugs.

And my dog, Nytra. She was smart. In fairly short order she figured out that when she smelled the drugs she was suppose to sit. That was a great feeling, seeing the light bulb click on in her head that she's suppose to sit to get the reward.

One of the things I learned handling a narcotic-detector dog is that you can't get embarrassed easily. The dogs are going to do things that embarrass you. Nytra was very strong willed. She wanted to do things when she wanted. So if it meant chasing groundhogs behind the Calgary Airport Detachment or ignoring my yelling and pleading to not dive into the mud puddle before going in to search a freshly cleaned hotel, she did what she chose. This became more and more problematic, as she started to follow her own interests during searching too. I would be doing everything I could to get her interested in the searching, but she'd just walk away and do what she wanted. When she felt like it, she'd come and smell what I was pointing to. Searching was extremely exhausting for me, as I had to be ultra animated to gain the slightest interest from Nytra.

I knew that Nytra's days as a drug dog were numbered the morning we came to get our dogs at the kennels and saw a fifth dog; a yellow Labrador retriever who was a nervous wreck, shedding like mad and hiding in his dog house. We were all interested in this newcomer, and we tried to coax him out and give him a welcome pat and scratch (something we don't do with the attack dogs), but he was just too timid.

Later that week, I traded my Nytra for the yellow lab, Dutch. That was a heartbreaking process. One day you are giving all your effort and love to your drug dog in training, and then the next day you walk past your old dog and take out a new dog. Even now it's hard to think of how Nytra looked at me as I coaxed Dutch out of his kennel to begin his training.

So, three and a half weeks into our eight week course, I was back to square one. The other teams were looking at getting ready for their first test, while I was back to trying to bond with my dog. Luckily, male dogs are much simpler creatures. Dutch and I bonded quickly, he was happy to have a buddy, he loved to play, and was really friendly once he go over his travel nervousness.

Unfortunately, Dutch wasn't meant to be my drug dog either. His animal tracking instincts were way too overpowering. Like Nytra, he learned the drug game very quickly and even with only two weeks training was already sitting when he found drugs. The fact that I already had some idea of what was expected of me surely helped. But I had to pre-search the drug search areas for any kind of animal distraction. Even a dead mouse in a trap on the other side of the room would be too wonderful a smell for

Dutch to ignore. There was once a dead bird outside a fire hall we were searching and that was it—I couldn't even get him in the door.

The deciding moment for Dutch was when we took the dogs swimming. We had the dogs in the pond and when it came time to go, the other dogs followed their handlers' command to come, the van was loaded and waiting for Dutch and me.

The problem was that Dutch had found a Canada goose. He crashed into the water towards the bird. It was a good fifty metre swim to the middle of the pond where the goose was floating. But Dutch was going to swim it; he was going to get the goose. Retriever breeds are water dogs and have webbed feet, like a duck, that help them swim. A goose, as it turns out, swims better than a dog. Dutch would swim toward the goose and it would just give a couple powerful kicks with its truly webbed feet and glide out of reach of Dutch. This continued for twenty minutes.

Bob, our trainer, was furious. I did everything I could: I called him and called him, Greg went and got Dodger to see if Dutch would come to another dog, I threw my ball into the pond hoping Dutch would call off the chase for an easier target. Nope, he was a bird dog and this was his calling. This was his moment to be everything that nature made him to be.

Bob was a former Emergency Response Team member (the RCMP version of SWAT). I saw him, in the distance, do that lean—that change of posture that a cop does when they are thinking about accessing their firearm. Bob went back to the van, with his pistol holstered. To this day, I don't know if Bob was thinking of shooting the goose or Dutch.

By now, Dutch was exhausted but not giving up the chase. As he became more and more spent he started to take in water and make drowning noises...yet he wouldn't stop.

The goose still refused to fly away, kicking casually to keep in front of Dutch. At one point the goose cruised by me as I was standing uselessly on shore, and flashed me a glance that seemed to say, "Is this yours?"

It was really starting to look like Dutch was going to drown. I peeled off my vest and dropped my gun belt as I was working out how I could rescue a drowning dog without getting bit. That's something they didn't cover in my National Lifeguard Service course. Just before I went in, I saw an opportunity. There was a big rock on the shore that I grabbed and launched into the water near the goose. It made a deep splash that scared the goose enough that it flew to the other side of the pond. With the goose finally out of sight, Dutch limped his way to shore. He was done. I really liked Dutch, he was a good loyal dog—clearly as dumb as a fence post, but loveable just the same.

I thought that was it for me, they were going to send me home because there wouldn't be enough time to train another dog. With Bob retiring, I was told that they would roll me into the next course if something like this happened, but I knew there was some reshuffling going on at the detachment while I was away, and if I went back to Toronto without a dog the detachment would likely cut their losses and I would never come back to the dog program.

Two days later, there was a little chocolate lab in the kennel. The day after that, Dutch's short police-dog stint was over and I was onto Fred. Dutch, I am sure, is now a stellar hunting dog somewhere, who is likely the pride and joy of his owner. There is no doubt that if Dutch could have caught that goose, he would have brought it back like a champ.

At this point it was the beginning of June. Just about three weeks left before Bob retired. And Fred and I were starting at the beginning. The others in the group had moved on through their first validation and were onto more advanced work, like searching bags on a moving carrousel and in people's pockets.

The others had their ups and downs too. Dodger, the untrained and insane golden that was paired with Greg had the light switch go on. It happened just like that too, one day, right in the middle of a search, Dodger just started to follow Greg's commands. By the end of the course Dodger was the best sniffer, still completely insane, but he knew the game and would be able to pick off drug hides from quite a distance.

Tank, with about three weeks left, had his light switch go off—again, right in the middle of a search. Craig was doing a luggage search, where the luggage was all laid out. At that point in training, a static luggage search was the easiest there was. Tank just stopped in the middle of the search and refused to go on. Craig was sweating bullets—that was really late in training to replace a dog. He fought hard though and got Tank through the course. Tank now holds a couple of records, including being the only police dog on anti-anxiety medication. But he was also prolific in finding dope, even getting a drug bust his very first day of service!

Trent and Levi pretty much slam dunked the course and went on to catch lots of drug couriers together. They made it look easy, but it was really a combination of Trent's skill and Levi's natural ability. They were a good team.

And Fred? He wasn't meant to be my dog either. They found a dog that was partially trained; with the time left they thought it would be better to switch my dog. Memphis, a female black lab was on her way. Fred went back to his owner in British Columbia, and I started with Memphis.

It was true. Memphis already knew the game. The RCMP purchased her from a trainer in California who got her from a family that couldn't handle her as she was just too nuts. So, naturally, she became a police dog in the RCMP.

It took a little bit to bond with Memphis. Having been abandoned, re-trained, and moved from one spot to another several times, she was unsure of people. When she arrived in Alberta, she was quite sick and didn't want to eat for a few days. Her early days of training took extra effort. The work was worth it. Memphis was to be my drug dog. We were able to bond, and she passed her first level of training in just a week. It helped that I had been through the early stages several times and could work at Memphis' level.

She was still an RCMP police dog. Her quirks were being discovered daily.

I discovered that when she got excited she would honk like a goose, which would be a comical introduction as we entered search areas during training, it was even better when it was a busy mall or airport. Also, she had an unnatural obsession with reflecting light, if a door opened and the sunlight moved across the floor, we'd have to wait until she finished chasing the light to get back to the job. I also discovered that she loved (or possibly really hated) stuffed animals, and would need to destroy any plush in her path. And, later I discovered that she liked to sing to Blackie and the Rodeo Kings, howling in time with the music.

So, with my wonder-dog Memphis we all graduated on time and we parted ways to go out and do our best to interfere in the criminal goals of drug runners, each of us proud to be RCMP dog handlers.

Editor's Note:
Corporal George Voelk is still a dog handler in Toronto, Ontario. Nash, a bomb detection dog, served through several elections, the "Toronto 18" investigation, the Olympics, and the G20. She is retired now and living with a very lucky and well protected family in Ontario. Constable Greg

Hawkins and Dodger are still in service near Edmonton, Alberta. Dodger is still nuts, and still a great police dog. Constable Trent Sperlie is working in the Regina, Saskatchewan drug section. Levi is retired, and is living with the civilian family who originally donated him to the RCMP. Constable Craig Webb is still hunting for drug couriers on the highways in Manitoba. Tank, although not an active drug dog anymore, is a very popular guest D.A.R.E.* presenter in Manitoba grade six classrooms. Tank still lives with Craig. Sergeant Bob Lowe retired the very day we became dog handlers, having served Canadians and the Police Dog Service program with distinction. Memphis and I are still in service in Toronto, Ontario. She still honks and she still sings and she is still often grumpy, but she finds drugs just fine.

* Drug Abuse Resistance Education, see DARE.com for more information

DAD'S BEER
Corporal Sandy McKechnie
Red Deer, Alberta

In Spruce Grove, Alberta the saying was, "It is so quiet that dead dogs bark at strangers." In the 1980s, Spruce Grove was pretty slow. As a posting, there was lots of time to make your own work.

I was on patrol one slow night trying to drum up any kind of action I could. With any luck I'd come across a drug deal or see a wanted person on the street and be able to make an arrest.

Rolling up to the intersection of King Street and Brookwood Drive, I noticed a couple of figures in the shadows lurking beside the corner store. I wheeled into the parking lot, being sure to keep an eye on them.

I saw one person place an item behind a dumpster while the other approached the car. Initially, these two seemed pretty street-wise. It is a common tactic; one person distracts the cop while the other drops the evidence. They weren't quite quick enough that night; I saw the second subject try to ditch the evidence.

"Hello constable," said the approaching subject. I could see that he was just a kid, maybe sixteen- or seventeen-years-old. I noticed that he was carrying a long necked, brown bottle. Still concerned about the apparent "distract and ditch" technique, I kept an eye on the other kid as I talked with the first kid through the open window of the police car.

"Hello there," I said. "That must be Dad's." I was referring to Dad's Root Beer that comes in long, brown, beer-style bottles. Seeing how he was outside a corner store, I figured he just bought the soft drink. I engaged him in trivial conversation to see what explanation, if any, he was going to offer up on his own as to why they were skulking in the shadows.

"No, it's mine," he said.

I looked at him for a long moment, confused by his answer. Then I saw that it was in fact a beer. I burst out laughing. I was so used to the lies that people tell when caught in such circumstances that his outright honesty caught me totally off-guard.

The kid didn't know that he couldn't just walk around town with a beer, let alone up to a marked police car.

But honesty goes a long way with me. I had the other kid retrieve his beer from behind the dumpster and rather than ticket them for a liquor offence, I just had them pour out their beer. I didn't have the heart to charge them.

For Spruce Grove, that is what had to pass for action and adventure that night. I found it pretty funny, and after thousands of investigations through my career, this is a story that I still enjoy telling.

THE MAJOR PROJECT
Constable James King
Newmarket, Ontario

I have often wondered what my life as a Mountie would be like if I could live it as a TV cop-show hero. The contrasts between what we see on TV and the reality of policing is so different that I find it hard to believe that the cop shows are even aired.

Recently, I investigated an importation of opium into the Toronto area. Opium is the raw tar that is harvested from the poppy plant. The tar can be smoked itself, or it can be processed into heroin. When legally manufactured, it is made into pain relievers like morphine. When on the streets, opium is very dangerous, as it is highly addictive.

On the TV cop show, the importation would go down something like this: a group of well-dressed men stand outside their dark cars, inside a warehouse, with a display of automatic weapons. They are surrounding a man with a slighter stature, clearly the person in charge. The group seems to be waiting for what feels like forever, as one of the well-dressed thugs lights a cigarette, trying to stay calm as they wait for their big moment. Finally, the garage doors open, revealing an expansive view of the night cityscape just as a motorcade of more cars speed in with a single, over-sized, tinted-out SUV coming up the rear. The huge doors of the warehouse are left open for the dramatic backdrop. More armed men file out of the convoy and take position facing the group already there. From the SUV appears a smaller man dressed to display his wealth. He approaches the apparent leader of the first group and they embrace like all bad guys do on TV. One of the men flashes the other an aluminum-clad briefcase. There is a quick check to make sure the content is cash, and the boss hands the briefcase to one of his thugs, and indicates that there is no need to count it. A show of the dope is made, so as to avoid any concerns that this is a rip-off. The briefcases are exchanged; the drug dealers all smile as they all feel like the drug deal has gone well.

Suddenly, dozens of cops storm the front of the building to arrest everyone. Hundreds of bullets are fired on both sides as the bad guys try to flee; the only bullet to make its mark is the bullet that hits the tire of the SUV, as it flees through the open cargo door. The vehicle lands in the bay, spilling its dope out for all to see. The driver escapes. One or two of the cops, and maybe a handful of drug dealers, are wounded in the massive shootout. Our TV cop-show hero walks to the edge of the pier and looks down at the sinking SUV, and says a cheesy one-liner like, "Not in my town."

The reality is that there is no Mr. Big that controls the drug industry. There are hundreds of independent groups that work together to help smuggle various drugs into Canada at various times, some groups being bigger than others. Even the big drug busts that are mentioned on the TV news seldom cause a dent in the illegal drug trade...it is that prolific!

Safe it to say, my investigation was a little more "blue collar" than our hero's investigation. The shipment was intercepted quietly in a warehouse by a heads-up border services officer (BSO) who thought the declared goods being shipped were too cheap to go through the added expense of being shipped by air. A closer look at the shipment showed the declaration was inaccurate compared with what they were finding in the boxes. The BSO and some of his co-workers decided to randomly open some of the cans in the shipment and they hit pay-dirt! They found the drugs in cans wrapped in multiple layers of plastic. Don't get me wrong. We were all pretty excited about the find, but there were no flashy SUV's, dudes in suits, and certainly no spray of bullets.

Back to our TV cop-show hero: he finds a matchbook and part of a burnt driver's licence at the scene, and he's on his way to solving the crime. By the next day, he has a full work-up on the detachment LCD screens showing everything from the suspect's driver's licence to where the subject lived for the last fifteen years, right down to his favourite colour. One or two checks on the police computer can wield loads of information in TV land.

In the real world, if someone had tried to pick up the shipment we would have been much further ahead. But, no one came for the load so we had to start digging from scratch.

There are over thirty separate databases to access in a large investigation. And there's no central database that allows us to gather information from one computer. So, I got assigned the file and I started the slew of checks. There are people to help us for some of them, but there are several of the databases that need to be accessed individually. So there I was for two weeks, with my seventeen inch monitor, telephone, fax machine, and unmarked police car to go here and there to collect the routine background information needed to work-up the details of the start of the investigation. Most of these databases are text based, and to actually find a picture of a location or person is a huge find early in the investigation.

With the subjects identified, each of our team members had to take three suspects each and do their background checks. That might not sound like a lot of checks to do, but three subject checks translate into a lot of report reading and summarizing to boil the information down to the salient details. One of the subjects used some false information on their driver's licence and that temporarily side-tracked the investigator. Once the suspect's real information was found, the checks had to be done all over again to make sure we had the accurate information. Snags like that are common in large drug investigations, and they take real work and real time to get past them.

However, in my fantasy cop show world the investigation was going on perfectly. The hero has been able to get everything he has needed so far. But he runs into an impolite store owner who refuses to look up a key piece of information that is stored on a private company computer. He walks out and gruffly demands to his boss on his cell phone, "I need a warrant."

One commercial break later, a warrant is emailed to his cell phone and he shows it to the clerk and he has his information.

Meanwhile, during my investigation, an investigator on my team came to me and said, "We need a warrant." I said, "Ugh." In the real world, warrants take a lot longer than a commercial break. Depending on the warrant, it can take weeks of writing to get it signed by a judge. For my investigation, I needed the warrant to obtain the suspect's banking information. We can find out if a suspect has a bank account at a certain financial institution, but the courts have determined that the bank records themselves aren't something the police should be able to arbitrarily go through. Fair enough, I wouldn't want the police going through my bank records without a supportable belief that there was a crime, and that my bank account information held some sort of evidence to that crime.

So, one of the investigators had to spend a week writing the warrant in order to get that information. It was worth it though, it lead us to further information that advanced the file. One of my non-police friends told me once that having to write a warrant is like a speed bump for an investigation. I told him it's more like a four day detour.

The collecting of information is one thing, but analyzing that information is another. We had several leads to follow, but it took us some time to sift through the countless pages of information to eliminate the false trails from the ones which were authentic and or useful.

Now that we had our list of suspects, and a good deal of information on paper, we set out to get to know them and how they act in the real world.

Our TV cop-show hero, well he'd just put "a tail on them", which usually involves one cop following a suspect for days. Sometimes the TV cop conducts a stakeout, from the back of a van or from a conveniently abandoned factory from across the street of wherever the suspect lives. Or the cop might have an informant who knows all the inside information into who was behind the shipment. Within a couple of days, he'd know where the drugs are being stashed, the residences of all his suspects, and the drug trade routes for the whole city.

The real process is much more complicated. I am not going to tell you the actual investigative steps we took to close in on the suspects. We still have our secrets. But rest assured our successes were rooted in hard work and long hours from dedicated police officers rather than any flashy, false heroism involving one cop following someone for days on end.

Take down day! Our TV cop show team is doing it in style: helicopters, a foot chase, and a two-part car chase that wrecks half the city. In the end, everyone is caught or dead. Our hero takes a bullet, but it's only to the shoulder and he was able to shrug it off long enough to fight the last bad guy hand to hand and to knock him unconscious with his good arm. His boss, who had been riding him the whole time, now with everyone shot or captured, with the whole city on fire, is able to muster a half-hearted, "Good job."

Take down days are exciting, even in the real world. There's something about descending upon totally unaware suspects and making the arrests. We had the required warrants (yes, more warrants) that allowed us to enter and search the apartment and to arrest the suspect. We set-up in the hallway and were ready to slam the door with a door-ram that we affectionately call the "Key to the City". Those few seconds between being ready and getting the "go" order felt like a year. I could hear my heart pounding in my ears as the anticipation welled for the entry. We knew we'd likely find drugs in the apartment, and we're always worried about weapons. Even if someone in the apartment runs for the kitchen and gets a knife it can get ugly. Just getting into a fight with someone involving no weapons at all can lead to serious injuries. I know a lot of police officers that have bad backs or knees resulting from difficult arrests. Caution is always warranted.

The team leader whispered hastily, "GO! GO! GO!"

The Key to the City was a perfect fit and the door flew off its hinges. We stormed in and spread throughout the apartment. Everyone was arrested before anyone could make mad-dashes to get weapons, destroy evidence or make phone calls to their criminal buddies to warn them. In the apartment we found drugs and drug smoking paraphernalia. The air ducts and vents were taped up so smells wouldn't escape the apartment, drawing unwanted suspicion; that was a great little piece of evidence to their knowledge and intent to commit the drug crimes.

This is only half the story. The arrests trigger the court process. In this day and age in Canada, even simple cases take months to bring to trial and sometimes even as long as four or five years. All aspects of the investigation have to be disclosed; boxes and boxes, and DVD after DVD of information are released to the court and the accused outlining our roles and our techniques. The courts download more and more of the grunt work of disclosure to the police, even to the point of ordering paper copies of disclosures so the lawyers can more easily read the documents, compared to the highly organized DVD of data provided to them by the police already.

Our cop-show hero? Well, he just shows up at court with his one page of notes in his pocket sized book and is able to give all the evidence he needs. The prosecution throws in a surprise witness, there is a breakdown on the stand and it's all over.

Actual justice takes a little more care; as much effort as it takes to track down suspected criminals, they are just that, suspects. It is up to the courts to render a decision if they are actually guilty of the crime. The standard to convict should be very high. The thought of sending someone to jail who is not actually guilty is my worst nightmare, and such an event would undo all the effort and good intention of my work and is never my hope.

Our drug dealers, after receiving the volumes and volumes of evidence, decided to plead guilty in hopes of a better sentence. I always look at a guilty plea as a credit to the investigation. Importing opium brings a maximum sentence of life in prison. They were sentenced to seven years, and will likely be on parole (serving the rest of their sentence out in public) in two years—depending on their previous records. We will have spent longer on the investigation and administration of the case than they will in jail. But that is for others to concern themselves with really. I am an investigator, the lawyers, juries, and judges are responsible for the courts.

I wish I had the resources that the TV cop-show hero has at his disposal. The reality is that even with all the work the case could fall apart and all our efforts can be for naught. We try not to get too frustrated because we know that if we can't catch a criminal in a current investigation, we know they'll be caught later. The TV cop has to get things wrapped up in one hour, (unless it is serious enough for a two part episode). The Mounties will get our criminal because we can be methodical and patient.

WEDDING CAPERS
Charley Massey, Chaplain
Comox Valley, British Columbia

I'm not sure what causes it, but every time I celebrate the wedding of an RCMP member something out of the ordinary is bound to occur. Perhaps it has to do with the nature of their work: always being alert, on their toes, dealing with people experiencing problems, all the while suppressing their own emotions. This "something out of the ordinary" could also be related to their collective sense of humour coupled with a predisposition toward practical jokes.

Not too long ago, I attended a formal RCMP regimental dinner in the officers' mess at Canada Forces Base (CFB) Comox. One of the attendees, an RCMP officer, when he found out that I was an RCMP chaplain, told me a story about the wedding of his youngest brother, also a member, which had taken place fifteen years earlier and three thousand miles away.

Several members of the wedding party, on the groom's side, were also RCMP members and they liked to take a wee "nip of the spirits" once in a while to steady their nerves. The groom's brother, being a resourceful RCMP member, took on the task of reconnaissance of the church to see where the best spot would be to hide a little whisky. It would, of course, be used only in the case of emergency.

He found a spot, a place where it would stay cold too, and wouldn't need any ice. Where else would anyone hide a bottle, but in the toilet tank in the men's washroom? He wedged the stopcock open slightly so the water would constantly run, thus keeping the tank's precious contraband at the proper drinking temperature.

He had not counted on the minister needing to use the facility prior to the wedding. Most clergy who plan ahead go to the washroom last thing before a service; the practice often saves "problems" for the minister during the service. The pastor, a former Toronto Police Service member, stepped in to use the facilities. Finding the water running in the tank, he pulled the top off to correct whatever the problem might be. Needless to say he found the offending object.

Being a former policeman himself, he quickly zeroed in on the top cop in the wedding party and asked him if he knew anything about the bottle in the toilet tank. As if under oath he readily admitted guilt. They had a good laugh.

After hearing the story, I inquired as to where and when this had taken place. The RCMP officer told me but he couldn't remember the minister's name; but he did remember that prior to going into the ministry he had been a police officer. I described the physical features of an individual whose name had come to mind, and he immediately replied, "That's him! Do you know him?"

Did I know him? We had shared accommodations while at seminary in the late 60s and early 70s (ten years before the aforementioned wedding) and we are still very good friends. I was going to have some fun with this.

The morning after the dinner I phoned my former roomie. Phone calls back and forth were fairly frequent, so it was not a surprise to him that I would be calling. After asking about families and weather, I told him I was very concerned about certain activities of which I had heard, particularly those surrounding a certain wedding which he had celebrated.

He asked what I was talking about, and I told him that he was the only minister I knew who hid booze in the toilet tanks of churches for the convenience of nervous wedding parties. I can still picture him falling off his chair as he broke into fits of laughter, inquiring, between bursts, as to where I had heard the story. When I told him, he even filled me in on further details the original narrator had neglected to tell me.

This parson assured me, in no uncertain terms, that it only happened once. But then, one never knows what individuals in wedding parties will have planned, especially RCMP wedding parties.

Another RCMP wedding caper had the appearance of "ALF" at a wedding. That's ALF, as in alien life form from the television series popular in the late 1980s.

The bride, the groom, the best man, the ushers, and the father of the bride were all RCMP members from across the country. As they left the church after the rehearsal, the groom was tackled by the wedding party. He had his identification, money, credit cards, and other valuables taken away, and he was dressed in an ALF costume. The bride's purse was confiscated for safe keeping.

The bride and groom were then handcuffed together and placed on an Ottawa city bus. Their fare was paid and they disappeared into the maze of local traffic patterns. They rode for a while trying to figure how they were going to get out of the predicament in which they found themselves.

They eventually got enough transfers to arrive at the office of the local constabulary where they explained their tale of woe. For some strange reason their story was believed and they found their freedom.

I knew that this little caper was going to take place. Subconsciously, not wanting to be totally left out, I discovered a plan was developing in my own mind.

I had in my possession a teddy-bear wearing a T-shirt with a police crest on it and the words, "The Police Chaplain Cares About You." Now, I also had an ALF stuffed toy which, by coincidence, had the same measurements as the teddy-bear. It was only logical that ALF, wearing the police chaplain T-shirt, should attend the wedding. He sat through the service on top of the organ at the front of the church.

About halfway through the service the bride suddenly noticed ALF. It wasn't long before the whole wedding party were trying extremely hard to maintain decorum so we could finish the wedding.

Between the signing of the register and the wedding party retiring down the centre aisle, the wedding party broke out in laughter over the unexpected guest and his reminder of the events the day before. I had the pleasure of explaining the sudden laughter to the congregation, so they could share in the joke.

In my photo file, I have a picture taken at the front of the church with me between the bride and groom, with the bride holding ALF.

Like I said, with a Mountie wedding, you just never know for sure what's going to happen. But you know it's going to be memorable.

SWALLOWERS
Constable Aaron Sheedy
Toronto, Ontario

There can be no other way to look at it. The "Super Loo" brings clarity to the fact that there isn't much further to slip in one's life.

Deep in the bowels of Terminal One at the Lester B. Pearson International Airport in Toronto are the RCMP cells; and at the very back of the cells is the stainless steel plumbing contraption known as the Super Loo. Looking at this device, you wouldn't immediately come the conclusion that it is in fact a toilet; a toilet with the sole purpose of filtering swallowed drug packages from the excrement of the courier. The device is a case of function-murdering fashion in cold blood. There is nothing at all redeeming or complimentary about its looks.

All the surfaces are a cold stainless steel. The bowl, as such it is, is a square hole that leads to an internal stainless steel chamber where the drug packages are collected. This chamber has two holes that are covered by industrial rubber gloves that allow sterile access to the drugs in the chamber. The plumbing for the Super Loo is mounted on the outside of the wall for easy access because everything leaks all the time. Needless to say, when a drug courier mounts the Super Loo to do their business, the Mountie on duty isn't witnessing the courier's finest hour. And don't think that Mountie isn't having a gut-check on his or her career choice either. The drug packages still have to be retrieved; the system is far from automatic.

In late 2002, I was posted to the Federal Enforcement Section (FES) at the Toronto Airport Detachment. We were responsible for the Lester B. Pearson International Airport. It was my first post in the RCMP. Quickly my eyes were opened to the lengths people would go to bring drugs into Canada; I dealt with scores of couriers and investigated every imaginable importation method. Our counterparts at the Canada Border Services

Agency were making bust after bust, night after night. It fell to our little section to seize the dope, deal with the couriers, do the investigations, and take the cases to court. In the early days there were many around-the-clock shifts.

Also in those days, the Super Loo was used daily.

Typically drug couriers aren't sophisticated criminals. Largely, they get paid to take the risk of getting caught at the border. Whether the drugs are tied to their bodies, hidden in food or constructed into false sides of suitcases, they have come to a point in their life where they are willing to take the risk of years in jail for about three thousand dollars.

But someone who is willing to swallow a half kilogram of cocaine in a hundred, five gram pellets to be crapped out later is a whole different level of desperate. Swallowers are, in my mind, very much criminals, selfishly bringing in drugs that destroy lives for their own profit, but they're also, to some degree, victims.

It typically takes three days for a swallower to pass all their pellets. During that time, they stay at the RCMP cells at Pearson Airport. Because of the length of stay and the nature of their incarceration (multiple supervised trips to the Super Loo), there are lots of opportunities to get to know the prisoners. There are several memorable interactions with swallowers that come to mind.

There was one man who was very forthcoming about his knowledge of the drug importation rings in Toronto. As I walked him down the hall to the Super Loo, we were discussing the merits and detractions to the various importation methods available. He positioned himself on the Super Loo and prepared to make his deposit. He paused, looked at me thoughtfully and said, "I really think all the smart people are swallowing." It was all I could do not to laugh out loud.

There was the man who insisted on doing his business entirely naked. We strongly suggested that he at least wear his shoes, but no. He could only "go" naked. So three or four times an hour, he took the walk to the Loo, without any shame whatsoever, in his birthday suit.

Sadly, we were regulars at the Etobicoke General Hospital and I am sure the nurses, x-ray techs, and doctors have their share of swallower stories. In my time, there were at least six swallowers who had emergency surgery to have obstructed pellets removed from their bowels. Some like to simplify the risk of what will happen to a person if five grams of almost pure cocaine is released in their digestive track by saying, "It is the risk they took." But when you witness it first hand and are present for their last words, and then explain it all to their loved ones, that risk becomes pretty one-sided.

One weekend in the summer of 2003, we were doing our usual shift at Pearson. We had three swallowers at once all of whom were on the same flight arriving from Jamaica.

Martin and Shawn were arriving in Canada as part of the Farm Worker Program. This program is a win-win situation for the participants. The farm owners get labour at a rate that is more affordable than Canadian wages and the workers get wages that are better than what they get at home, often being able to support their families for the year with the wages they get from the few months of harvest in Canada.

Martin was a preacher at his local church and, by being part of the Farm Worker Program, didn't need to search out other work in Jamaica. He would also pastor the other workers while in Canada. He was considered one of the leaders of the group.

Shawn was a family man. He had two kids and a wife, and prided himself on being able to take care of them by doing this work. He had been doing it for eight years.

We immediately keyed in on the pair. We knew if two of the most experienced workers were importing, there had to be others; there would have to be an overseer who was in charge of everything, and who had likely arrived with them. There would have to be a plan to afford the group of swallowers the privacy to pass their pellets over the next couple of days and pass the drugs off to someone here in Canada. This was very much a crime in progress.

As we interviewed the pair, we did everything we could to drive the weight of their crime home. We were betting that they were good people who had had a horrible lapse in judgment. We showed them every angle of their mistake—the risk to them, their families, to their reputations—in the hopes that they would try to make it right and put us on the trail of the other criminals. By the end of the interviews they were exhausted. Shawn, in particular, was a mess.

In 2003, the RCMP cells were in the old Terminal One at Pearson Airport. These facilities were far from modern. The cellblock was one row. There were five or six rooms including the three cells, the interview room, and the Super Loo at the end of the hall. It was cramped, it smelled, and sounds of Shawn sobbing uncontrollably echoed loudly throughout the cellblock. I can only imagine the fear that Marcus felt as he was marched in and given his requisite tour of the Super Loo.

Marcus was younger, a nineteen-year-old Canadian living in Toronto. He had family in Jamaica and was down there for a funeral, or that is what he told the border services officer who interviewed him. It didn't take long for Marcus to talk himself into a corner and end up admitting that he swallowed drugs. Marcus wasn't dumb, he wasn't really even that simple. I was having a hard time understanding how he came to be a drug swallower. Marcus was lodged into the cell right beside Shawn. Shawn's cries echoed through the entire cellblock.

By the next day, Shawn's sobs had decreased in volume but were still pretty much full-time. There was a constant rotation up and down the hall between the three prisoners. Neither Martin nor Marcus complained about the constant noise despite having good cause to.

I can't say we were sorry we took the statement—the people of Canada have a right to have crimes against them investigated aggressively—but we did feel some responsibility for the derailment of Shawn's condition. We decided to do what we could. We tried several things but none of them worked. I could hear through his sobs that he was praying, which was more of a pleading really so we brought him a copy of the Bible, but he couldn't read. That idea was a bust. We put music on in the cell hallway. We brought tea, we tried to talk to him and discuss the court process that he faced with the hope that, if he understood what was going to happen, he might calm down. None of it worked.

We came to the conclusion that this had gone on long enough and that perhaps the airport nurse should become involved. She came and left refusing to provide any medication because she didn't know what reaction it may have with the possible cocaine in his system.

It had been almost two solid days.

My partner had the idea of putting him in touch with a loved one in Jamaica. I was up for the idea; perhaps a friendly voice would do the trick. It made matters even worse. It ended in even more uncontrolled sobbing. My partner was on the phone for fifteen minutes explaining to Shawn's panicked wife that he was safe and that everything was being done to get the drugs out safely. What a disaster.

Through this whole time Marcus remained quiet, didn't ask for anything and did everything we asked of him.

Finally Martin and Shawn had passed all their pellets and it was time to transfer them into the court system. It was the middle of the night and we're almost certain the receiving jail wouldn't accept Shawn in his current state. We were discussing taking him to the hospital, when Martin banged on his door. "Let me talk to him," he said in his heavy Jamaican accent.

We theorized it couldn't go worse than the call home so we allowed Martin into Shawn's cell. Shawn immediately started to wail about his wife, his kids, and how he was in trouble with the police. Martin startled us when he yelled at Shawn.

"Is God going to forgive you?" Shawn tried to keep crying. Martin demanded again, "Will God forgive you?"

Shawn squeaked out a, "Yes."

"Then no man should hold the grudge. It is time to go set this right." said Martin.

Shawn pulled himself together and didn't shed another tear. We all took some quiet time. The only sound was a quiet, "Amen." from Marcus' cell when everyone realized that the sobbing was over.

The next night I relieved the day shift. Marcus was the only prisoner and I took over supervising his last few trips to the Super Loo. During the day he had declined to give a formal statement, but during our second walk down the hall he struck up a conversation.

"Crazy couple of nights, eh?" he started. It was like he wanted me to know he was different than the other two. I knew he was, I still really wanted to know how he ended up a swallower. So I asked.

Marcus lost his job the same week that his girlfriend told him he was going to be a father. He had always worked and took pride in being able to afford what he wanted: a car, a shared apartment, and money for evenings out with his friends.

Marcus' father always worked hard and Marcus looked up to him for that. So when he hit the rough patch, he went to visit his father in Jamaica.

"I asked him," Marcus said, "How did he always manage to keep it together with one job and three kids?" Marcus got quiet, like he was holding back anger. "Then, then that's when he told me about this."

Marcus' father would work as much as he could, but when the ends weren't meeting, he'd go visit his mother in Jamaica and come back with a belly full of cocaine. After a week of his father explaining that swallowing was how his family was able to make ends meet, Marcus decided to do it.

It seemed obvious, but I had to tell him that I thought it was a tremendous risk, not only the risk of getting caught, but the very real risk of dying if a pellet bursts.

"It's one of those things that seemed like a good idea at the time," Marcus said. "But no offence, I don't ever want to come back here again." A couple of hours later, Marcus was off into the court system with all of his pellets safely passed.

I never saw Martin and Shawn again. I heard that they pled guilty at the very first opportunity. In fact they tried to plead guilty to the justice of the peace at their bail hearing. They were sentenced and they spent their time in a Canadian prison. They were both granted early release and were deported directly from prison. As far as I know, they are both free men now but they can't ever come back to Canada or the United States. They had it good here and they took a terrible risk and lost. At least they never blamed anyone other than themselves for their lot.

I saw Marcus once more. He too pled guilty and offered no excuse other than an apology to the court. He was sentenced and I met him at our office two years later when he came to collect some of his belongings. He had gotten a job at an auto parts plant in the area after he was released. He told me that he was making good money and had benefits for his daughter.

The Super Loo brings people to rock bottom very quickly, but Marcus shows that you don't have to live there. He shook my hand, looked me in the eye, and told me to take care of myself before he walked confidently out of the detachment.

HAPPY BIRTHDAY, REALLY?
Staff Sergeant Bob MacAdam
Newmarket, Ontario

I've been a police officer for almost forty-two years now, eight and a half with the Toronto Police Service (1969 to 1977) and thirty-three and a half with the RCMP (1977 to 2011). Like every other cop, I have been involved in all manner of incidents and investigations, some tragic and sad, many routine, and some which, despite a serious aspect, are memorable because they were funny or unusual, sometimes to the point of being almost unbelievable. This tale is of the latter variety, and when thinking back over my career, this story always comes to mind.

It occurred in 1982 when I was posted in Bay Roberts Detachment in the province of Newfoundland and Labrador (known in the RCMP as B Division). The town of Bay Roberts is a small town in Conception Bay North, about an hour from the capital city of St. John's. Within the Bay Roberts Detachment area were a number of communities of various sizes. The detachment was staffed by nine RCMP members—a sergeant, a corporal and seven constables. We also had one detachment clerk and a number of other part-time employees (including jail guards, matrons, auxiliary constables, cleaners). We weren't the smallest in the division, but we were pretty small.

We were busy, but in a different way than my days with the Toronto Police Service. In Toronto, the uniform police constables (PCs as we were called) spent most of our time responding to calls for service. We dealt with numerous calls every shift, made a lot of arrests, and did cursory investigations of the more routine matters. At the end of the shift, we would hand in our investigative reports and any of the criminal investigations would go to the detective office for follow-up. The mandate of uniform PCs was not to investigate but rather to patrol and to respond to calls for service.

I quickly found that life in small town Canada as an RCMP member was entirely different. We spent a fair bit of time patrolling and responding to calls for service, but it was also our role to investigate the various complaints. Bay Roberts was a busy detachment and it was not unusual for the constables to carry anywhere from fifty to seventy investigative files at a given time. This number would include thefts, assaults, warrants of committal, motor vehicle accidents, break and enters, sexual assaults, sudden deaths, damage complaints, liquor offences, impaired driving offences, frauds, and a variety of other occurrences. It was virtually impossible to do our work and do it well without working "voluntary overtime". Our members were a dedicated group and they routinely worked forty to one hundred hours of unpaid overtime monthly just to keep up with the heavy workload.

Despite the workload, the morale was great, the people in the communities were friendly and supportive (even to Mainlanders such as me) and I found it to be a fantastic experience. The thirteen years spent in various locations in Newfoundland and on the coast of Labrador were unquestionably the most memorable and enjoyable years of my life. I was transferred from B Division in 1990, but my wife is a Newfoundlander, two of my three children were born in that wonderful province, and I am what's commonly known as a "wannabee" (someone who wishes he was a Newfoundlander).

In the early 1980s, the fishery was still fairly strong in Newfoundland and many people in the out-ports were employed in the fishing industry. Having said that, unemployment was high in the out-ports and that, coupled with the fact that there weren't many activities to occupy one's time, contributed to the heavy drinking that was prevalent in rural Newfoundland. This is not meant in any way as a criticism, but was a reality. As a result, a large percentage of our time was spent investigating liquor offences and incidents involving drinking and driving.

That brings us to the events which prompted me to write this story. On Saturday, August 21, 1982, Constable Dominic Broaders (a Newfoundlander from Fogo Island) and I were working the 8:00 PM to 4:00 AM shift. There were only three or four of us in the area that weekend. One or two of the members were on holidays and the others were gone to the B Division slo-pitch softball tournament in Corner Brook on the west coast of the island. It had been a relatively quiet Saturday night and at approximately 1:45 AM (Sunday morning), we received a radio call to the effect that there had been a hit and run accident in Marysvale (a very small community about twenty minutes southeast of Bay Roberts). We were told that a pedestrian had been struck by a car and that an ambulance was en route.

We learned that a young man named Ambrose had been celebrating his birthday and to finish off his evening, he had walked to the home of his brother, Ron where they had a couple of beers to commemorate the occasion. At about 1:30 AM, Ambrose left his brother's place and began walking home. The road was narrow and dark and the shoulders did not allow much room for pedestrians. He hadn't gone very far when an approaching vehicle came flying around a bend in the road, hugging the shoulder. Ambrose was unable to get out of the way; he was struck by the car and thrown into the ditch suffering fairly serious injuries to his legs. The driver may or may not have known what he had done but, either way, the car continued on and disappeared out of sight over the hill. Despite his injuries, Ambrose was able to drag himself at least partially out of the ditch in the hope that someone would see him and assist him. As he lay there in pain, he had to be feeling somewhat sorry for himself and how his birthday had come to such a sorry ending.

If only he knew.

After just a few minutes however, another vehicle did come along and the occupants, Frank (the driver) and Russell (the passenger), stopped to help. They lifted him up into the front seat of Frank's car and drove up the road to Ron's house. Frank parked on the wrong side of the road and ran inside and told Ron that his brother Ambrose had been hit by a car and was injured. He told Ron to call the police and an ambulance. Meanwhile, Russell was standing beside Frank's car with the passenger side door open trying to reassure Ambrose, telling him that help was on the way and that he was going to be alright. Suddenly, a vehicle came over the crest of the hill at a high rate of speed and smashed head-on into Frank's car. Ambrose was tossed around inside the vehicle and sustained further injuries. The open door hit Russell and sent him flying into a field causing him some injury. The driver of the other vehicle went headfirst into the windshield knocking him unconscious.

Constable Broaders and I were en route to the location and a moment later, we received another call telling us about the second accident, the fact that more people had been injured and that a second ambulance had been dispatched.

We arrived at the scene a few minutes later and found one ambulance already there. The ambulance attendants were loading Ambrose into one ambulance and a moment later, the second ambulance arrived. Russell wasn't too seriously injured and he was put into the ambulance with Ambrose. The driver of the other car, a young university student named Tony was still unconscious and bleeding so they treated his wounds as best they could and put him aboard the second ambulance.

Both ambulances headed for St. John's via the Trans-Canada Highway with the injured parties. It's hard to say what was going through Ambrose's mind as he laid there heading for the city, but he had to be wondering how his special day could have taken such a turn for the worst. Oh well, he was in safe hands now and on the way to hospital.

At least, that's what he reasonably expected.

For readers not familiar with Newfoundland, you may not be aware of the large moose population in the province. That's great for hunters, but not so wonderful for people who use the highways. There are many vehicle-moose accidents annually and unfortunately some of them are fatal. As luck should have it, as Ambrose was lying in the ambulance on his way to St. John's, wondering how his birthday could have gone so horribly wrong, a large bull moose decided that he wanted to cross the Trans-Canada and he did so right in the path of the ambulance. The ambulance driver was unable to avoid a collision and our birthday boy was involved in an accident for the third time on this, the most memorable of all birthdays. Fortunately no one was seriously injured this time, although things did not go well for the moose. All hands eventually did make it to the hospital and everyone involved in this series of mishaps recovered from their injuries.

That was not the end to this incredible story though. Our investigation revealed that the vehicle that struck Ambrose when he was walking along the road was the same vehicle that crashed head-on into Frank's car (with Ambrose in it) a short time later. And of course, Tony was the driver both times. It was as though Tony was not satisfied with hitting Ambrose the first time and decided to come back and try to finish the job. Of course, that was not the case. Tony had been drinking heavily that night and was on his way to drop his girlfriend off at home when he hit Ambrose initially. In his intoxicated state, he continued on around the pond and safely delivered his girlfriend home (safely for her that is ... no one else in the vicinity was safe from Tony that night). Tony then drove back down the road and a combination of speed and his inebriated condition contributed to him hitting Frank's car.

Tony ended up being charged with some criminal code driving of-

fences. I don't know what penalty he received, but that really isn't important at this point, and it is not what makes this story memorable.

As August 21 comes and goes each year, I often think of Ambrose, and wonder what became of him. I'm certain that he has never had another birthday like that one almost thirty years ago, at least I hope not. With any luck, Ambrose has enjoyed good health, prosperity, and the companion-ship of a good woman. With what he endured on that one fateful night, he deserved good fortune for the remainder of his life.

SUMMER OF '77
Sergeant Rick Bigland (Ret.)
Penticton, British Columbia

In the summer of 1977, I was the junior constable, working in a three-man detachment in Beiseker, Alberta. Beiseker had one main street and was a typical small prairie town of about five hundred people. We policed a district that contained four other towns of about the same size. It was a pleasant district in which to work; the people were generally quiet, friendly, and very pro-police. We were located about eighty kilometres from the Calgary city limits. At the time I was twenty-four-years-old, recently married, and had one daughter. I had been in the RCMP for four years and it was my third posting, not uncommon for those days.

It was a very warm day in early July, and my shift was to end at 8:00 PM. At about 6:00 PM, I figured I had just about enough time to drive out to Carbon and make some enquiries on a break and enter file investigation that I started earlier. Carbon was a forty minute drive to the east of Beiseker. After getting about half way there, Calgary dispatch called on the radio. The dispatcher advised me there was a complaint from a farmer near Delacour, reporting that a couple of people were having a drinking party in one of his fields. The location was about thirty-five minutes south of Beiseker, or, just about an hour from where I was when I got the call.

I had heard on the radio, minutes earlier, that a highway patrol member, Alf, had dropped into Beiseker and gone for coffee at the senior constable's residence. Alf worked out of the Strathmore Detachment, but his area included Beiseker for highway duties. I called Alf and asked him if he was planning on returning to Strathmore via highway nine. Alf stated he was, and I asked him to check on the "party" on his way by Delacour. Alf said he would and I continued on to Carbon.

A few minutes later the dispatcher radioed Alf; there was a serious injury accident on the Trans-Canada Highway near Strathmore, and he needed to respond code three (as fast as possible). This, of course, meant my party complaint was still un-serviced. I debated with myself on what to do. The break and enter complaint was more serious than the party, but the party was in progress. Given the time it would take me to get to the party complaint there was a good chance the participants would be gone by the time I got there. Added into the mix was that attending the complaint would make me late for getting home to my family. The tipping point was that the dispatcher had mentioned that the people at the party were drunk and there was a blue pickup there. Failure to attend the call on my part might mean a drunk driver causing an accident. I decided I would at least have to make the effort.

I turned my patrol car around and headed south. Frustrated, I put my foot on the gas and went much faster than the priority of this call would normally require. In just over half an hour, I was travelling down the gravel grid road near the scene. The hot July air made heat waves rise above the front of the car and the gravel road made dust kick up behind me.

From the field entrance I could see the truck, an old blue one with a wood cap on the back. No people were visible. I pulled up to the driver's door of the truck which was about a hundred yards into the hay field, but I still could not see anyone. I began to think they had all left in another vehicle. I got out of the police car and walked up to the driver's door of the truck and looked inside. A male, just a little older than me was slumped over the seat and appeared to be asleep. I opened the door and shook him. He gave no response. Another shake got me a "fuck off" from the driver. I detected a heavy smell of booze. It appeared that he would not be too co-operative when he did wake up.

The complainant said it was a party so that would indicate there were more people. If they were as cranky as this guy, I might have had my hands full. So, I decided to take the keys out of the ignition and handcuff the semi-conscious drunk to the steering wheel so I wouldn't be double-teamed or jumped from behind while I looked for the others. And with me having his keys, he'd be where I left him when I got back. I walked around the back of the truck looking for the rest of the party.

About ten feet from the back passenger bumper of the truck was a female lying on the ground. She was naked with the exception of wearing an army-style brown jacket. She was young and had long, dark hair. Nearby, lay a roofer's hammer hatchet. Clearly the hammer had been used to beat her face until it was unrecognizable. Her eyes were swollen shut and her lips smashed. I could see no teeth in her mouth. It appeared that he had either cut or bit the rest of her body countless times.

When I kneeled down beside her she groaned and tried to turn away. I told her I was a police officer and that I was there to help her and would call her an ambulance. I do not know if she heard me or, if she did, what she was thinking. I went to my car and called for an ambulance and tried to describe the scene. I got an emergency blanket from the back of my police car and covered the girl. I again told her who I was and that help was coming. She made no reply. I thought of my first aid training, but she was breathing and the blood was coming from her head which had obviously been beaten. I didn't want to put a pressure bandage there for fear of doing more damage. I did what I could for her.

I went back to the truck. The male had woke-up and was staring at his handcuffed hand. I undid the handcuff from the steering wheel and fixed it to his other hand. I put him in the back of the police car. I noticed that his pants were undone in the front. I told him he was under arrest for assault and read him the police caution, advising him that he was under investigation and anything he said could be used as evidence against him in any criminal charges. He gave no response. I returned to the girl and told her again that help was coming. She made no sign that she heard me.

The ambulance was the first to arrive followed closely by the senior constable from Airdrie Detachment. The ambulance crew worked quickly and from the tone of their voices, I could tell her condition was not good. I remember one of them glaring at my prisoner in the back of the car. They told us that they could not get an IV into the girl as her veins were collapsing. The only thing they could do was try to transport her to the hospital, code three. She died at the Calgary city limits, in the back of the ambulance.

Her name was Cathy and she came from a small town in Ontario. She and a girlfriend had come out with the intention of working at the Calgary Stampede and then returning home. Her girlfriend got a job at the midway. Cathy told her she had gotten a job with a carpenter and that was the last they saw of her. She was eighteen-years-old.

After I finished writing up my notes and a report and processed the exhibits, I returned to Beiseker Detachment. I had been working for twenty-two hours but did not feel tired, and had a hard time getting to sleep. Like most police officers, while at the crime scene you are not thinking of any danger, horror, or about yourself. In short, you are too busy to think about your own feelings. Later—sometimes years later—you think more about what happened and what you might or could have done differently. I have often thought about the ten minute delay in my response while I continued to work on the break and enter file while highway patrol was dispatched to the "party" complaint. Those ten minutes were a lifetime for Cathy.

A few days later, the homicide section called and asked me to canvass the area on the route that the killer would have taken to get to the field, in case somebody had seen something. I thought it pretty unlikely, but did it anyway. The third house I stopped at was an acreage owned by a young couple. They had been out gardening that day. They saw the blue truck drive by. It appeared a girl fell out of the passenger side. The truck stopped. The driver got out. The girl appeared to have winded herself falling out since she did not resist as she was put back in the truck by the driver. A neighbour's car pulled up behind the truck. The truck drove away. This happened about two miles from the scene.

I spoke to the neighbour who pulled up behind the truck. He had seen the same thing as the young couple, but added that the driver appeared to kick the girl before he put her in the back of the truck.

I didn't ask either of them why they didn't call us right away. There didn't seem to be a point anymore. These were not bad people and they certainly did not know what was about to happen to the girl.

Forensic evidence collected proved beyond any doubt that the killer was the man in the truck. He was found guilty of manslaughter, rather than murder, due to his intake of marihuana and alcohol. During the trial he never looked up at me or any of the other witnesses. He sat at his table writing on a pad of foolscap. He did not have horns growing out of his head. He looked as normal as anyone else in the room. The only thing odd about him was he wore an earring. That was odd in 1977 for a guy.

I have worked on a dozen or more homicides since then. I have spent thirty-eight years in the RCMP and continue as a reservist. But I remember this day like it was yesterday.

Editor's note: Rick is Sara Clark's father. Her story is "A Job Well Done".

PART III

A TIME FOR ACTION

THE CHASE
Constable Curtis Jarvis
Gilles Bay, British Columbia

Seemingly, it was just the start of another shift in Princeton, British Columbia; I was working an evening shift and was responding to the usual calls for the area. It was March 25, 2007. I went to an accident scene and I got a "be on the lookout for" (BOLF) a mentally distraught guy headed to Saskatchewan to kill his family. I filed it in the back of my mind, erasing it from my computer. As the evening went on, I received a call of a domestic in progress in Hedley, a town fifteen minutes from Princeton. I had been there before and knew all the players at the residence.

Our suspect had kicked in the door of his ex-girlfriend's home, and she and her new boyfriend had chased him out onto the front lawn. I called for assistance from Penticton and asked for a police dog, as I knew the area was surrounded by bush and the suspect was a known runner. I also brought along a member who happened to be around the office after shift as backup. We all arrived to find the suspect had done just that—disappeared into the bush. The dog handler and his dog who had come from Penticton were in the lead; we began our extensive search of the area weaving in and out of the bushes and reporting to the members who were patrolling in town and around the home.

Soon into the search, an off-duty traffic member heard us on the radio as he was travelling through and offered his assistance. As he patrolled the local roadway in case we flushed out the suspect, he came across a GMC Jimmy parked by the side of the road with a lone male occupant. Figuring he might have been flagged down by the suspect or may even be the suspect, he approached it to question the individual. As he spoke to the male driver, the traffic officer noticed how nervous the driver was and, out of the corner of his eye, he spotted a handgun on the floor of the vehicle. Playing it cool, like it was a regular stop, he headed back to his car and called for backup. The dog handler and his dog and I piled into my vehicle and arrived on scene within a minute.

By this time the traffic officer had run the plate and found it came back to, of all things, the suicidal, mentally distraught guy headed to Saskatchewan to kill his family. We decided quickly that we were taking this guy into custody before he hurt himself or anyone else. I approached the passenger's side with my service pistol drawn; the traffic officer went to the driver window, and the dog-man to the rear. He was ordered out of the vehicle and we received no response. After a second command, the driver dropped the vehicle into drive and reached for the gun! Fearing for my life and the safety of the other officers, I opened fire, putting five rounds into the car as it sped away. My final round shot out the rear tire of the vehicle.

We all ran to our vehicles and the chase was on. It was like I was watching a *Cops* episode on TV. The offender was trying to attain high-speeds but was unable to, due to his flat tire. Sparks were coming off as the tire was worn down to the rim, but he just kept going. As we got closer to town, we received news that he had called 9-1-1 and was on the phone with our dispatcher, Justin Smith. The suspect claimed to have two loaded handguns in the vehicle and was going to take out anyone who got in his way. He was demanding the chase be called off and he be allowed to get away, or else! "Suicide by cop!"—one of the worst things an officer can hear. "Suicide by cop" is when a suspect forces the police into a situation where they have to shoot the suspect in order to save someone else's life. It is the intention of the suspect to be killed by the cops. At this point, we knew it wasn't going to be good.

Corporal Houben was called-out from home. He was ready to set-up a spike belt just outside of town. A spike belt is a metal strip of spikes that is long enough to cross a road, and is meant to take out the tires of a fleeing vehicle. It was deployed and the three remaining tires of the suspect's vehicle were deflated. Still the vehicle did not stop, even with all four tires peeled off and sparks flying from all four rims. Yet again, we received an update from dispatch telling us he was still making demands and saying the only way to stop him was to kill him.

It was decided that the vehicle needed to be stopped before it reached town, and that the driver should be brought into custody before someone was seriously injured or killed. The town of Princeton's downtown core had numerous busy gas stations, generally filled with lots of people, and we were fast approaching the town. I pulled my police truck up and around the lead pursuit vehicle and punched the gas. I veered my police truck at eighty kilometres per hour into the rear, left-quarter of the suspect's truck.

The suspect's vehicle skidded and spun around, but he pulled it out and continued on towards town. The poor police dog that was riding in the back and the dog-man who was riding beside me were both holding on for dear life. All they could do was "enjoy the ride".

As we reached the gas station on the main road in town, I again punched the gas pedal hitting the vehicle from behind. I drove his vehicle forward and into the empty parking lot of the Chevron station hoping it would spin out, but it didn't. He pulled away from me heading for the road again. I struck it again, this time in the right corner, and as I pushed the vehicle I could see the front entrance to the local paint shop and us getting closer and closer. Turning the wheel to avoid going through the front of the shop, in the distance I spotted the Esso gas station and its big metal sign right along the roadway. It was a way to stop him! I hit the gas shifting our vehicle to form a T that he could not escape from. I looked forward at the sign knowing this would definitely stop the vehicle if I hit it as hard as I could. I pushed the gas pedal to the floor but it was like watching something in slow motion on TV. In his hand I could see a gun; he was desperately trying to steer his vehicle, but he wasn't going anywhere.

I pushed my vehicle into the steel post wrecking both the post and my vehicle. I spun twenty metres from the suspect vehicle. I drew my firearm and tried to exit my vehicle. It had hit so hard that the front end was pushed back into the sides of the vehicle making my door almost impossible to open. I kicked at my door finally throwing it open. I could hear shots coming from the Esso parking lot. Corporal Houben had caught-up to us and had confronted the armed suspect in the parking lot.

Justin Smith, our dispatcher, was from the area and did a great job calling ahead and having all the local businesses close up and warn what customers they could. Unfortunately, the Esso station, where we were, was new and was the only place not notified. Our suspect, now shot in the arm, was inside the Esso with two hostages.

I circled around the station with the dog-man, securing the left and right side of the building. Others caught up to us securing the front. I looked around, peering into the front window, and could just see the suspect and two unsuspecting hostages in the window.

Now powerless, I stood there with my gun drawn ready for whatever might come, and all I could think was, "Holy shit!" I couldn't believe what had just happened and that it wasn't over. Every scenario played out quickly in my mind, but all I could do was to be vigilant and wait. I held my position for about an hour before other officers arrived.

They had begun a basic dialogue inside with the suspect from a base station at a local hotel and the first hostage was about to be released. The suspect who had been shot was demanding drugs and it was agreed that he would receive some painkillers in exchange for releasing a hostage.

As she came out, I jutted out and grabbed her by the arm bringing her around the building to safety. I quickly asked her questions pertinent to the incident at hand. Yes, it looked like a real gun and there was only one. Yes, there were only two hostages, the other one being her husband. And, there were no other way out other than the front door. I secured her in my police vehicle with an argument. She had only spent a little time with him, but she was already downplaying and sympathizing with the suspect's plight. I explained to her the seriousness of the situation and returned to my post as I didn't want to leave the gas station unsecured. Soon after backup arrived, I escorted our released hostage to the hotel room now staffed by the Emergency Response Team for debriefing.

I again returned to the scene and my post. With my adrenaline slowing and the rush gone, I was starting to feel the effects of my actions. My arm was sore, my neck was sore, and my back slowly started to clench up. Again more backup arrived coming from Keremeos, Penticton, and Merrit. I was ordered off scene and to the hospital.

Luckily I only received minor injuries, nothing that a week off and some medication couldn't fix. The hostage situation ended uneventfully eight hours later with the suspect finally giving himself up.

Later we found out that he had robbed a couple stores on his way to Princeton and was also responsible for a home invasion. We further found out there was a third hostage! An unsuspecting patron at the gas station had wisely holed himself up in the bathroom with no one knowing he was there until the Emergency Response Team swept the building.

This was my first major incident and I had no idea what to expect. I'm told I got the usual treatment by Major Crime. My gun was seized as evidence and I had to tell my story for hours with endless questions. I received a call soon after from the head of Major Crime. I received the company line right off the bat. He said, "You know you've done wrong, so you take what you have coming. You do not shoot at moving vehicles and you do not ram vehicles multiple times." Then in the same breath he said, "No one died or got hurt other than the bad guy so...good job." My punishment was to review policy and to talk to my boss at length. I took pride in knowing I did what I thought was right.

In September of 2008, the suspect pleaded guilty to a string of charges in Princeton, Merritt, and Calgary and received a federal jail sentence of fifteen years with twenty-five years to be spent under supervision. A surprisingly large sentence and a fitting end to what happened.

Figuring all was done, I moved on to my next post, of course retelling this story many times to many people. I was surprised to find an email in the summer of 2009 offering me congratulations for these events. It seems that Inspector Fudge of Penticton had put me up for a Commendation for a job well done. In November of 2009, I found myself at a dinner with Corporal Houben at Government House in Victoria. Our actions did not go unnoticed and we were both presented by the Lieutenant Governor and Solicitor General with medals of Valorous Service for, "acts of exceptional valour in the face of extreme hazard," British Columbia's highest honour for a police officer. In December of 2009, I then again found myself in Campbell River accepting a Commendation award from the RCMP, our highest honour.

As a member of the RCMP I don't expect any award. I do my job because it's what I have always wanted to do and I love doing it. But then again, it's always nice to be recognized for a job well done!

180 DEGREES
Sergeant Mirza Karimullah
Ottawa, Ontario

Part of the mystery of the RCMP is where you will be posted from Depot. In my day, they flat out told you that you would not get back to where home was for you. I was from Toronto—Brampton actually (a city just outside Toronto). In the academy, in Regina, Saskatchewan, they asked me to choose three of the provinces or territories where I'd like to go. I thought I would make it easy so I said, "I will happily serve anywhere—except Saskatchewan." The flatness of the land was depressing to me. Well, I suppose the RCMP felt I needed to appreciate the flat and rectangular province, because that's where they put me.

Yorkton, Saskatchewan, a fairly large city for the province, is where I landed. I learned to love the city and province in a hurry. It is a very welcoming community and a simply amazing detachment. There were very patient members there—having to deal with a city boy like me and all the city-boy-meets-small-town adjustments. For example, on patrol I once followed the dull glow of what I thought was a bush party that I could see off in the north, the lights from the fire reflecting off the clouds. What did I know about the Northern Lights? Dispatch left me hot on the trail of the aurora borealis for a while, but clued me in before I hit the Arctic Ocean. I learned there are finer skills not taught in the academy—skills that must be acquired in the field.

One September evening, I was on patrol after a fine mist of rain had ended an unusually warm, plus-two degree Celsius, Saskatchewan day. The sun was setting and it was getting a bit cooler. I was in a residential area familiarizing myself with my city. That is job one for all cops, know your area! I was miserably lost. My partner was in the area in his car watching me and laughing over the air every time I drove into a dead end, or signalled to turn where illegal. I was patrolling nice and slow to learn the layout. I knew I could use the map, of course, if a complaint came in so I wasn't worried about being lost. Fate had other plans however.

My partner radioed that he had spotted a suspect vehicle from an earlier criminal complaint—and he was only a few blocks away from me. The suspect car was not stopping for him (fleeing) and he requested backup. No time for a map. I radioed that I was on route and hit the lights and sirens. Now I wasn't speeding primarily because I was still a bit lost. Nonetheless I did accelerate from my crawling patrol cruise. What I didn't realize was that the fine mist of rain had turned to ice as the evening settled, creating a perfect skating rink on the road. There were no snow tires on the car yet, and back then traction control was a luxury not found on police cars. So the back end of the police car started to fishtail back and forth as I tried to correct with the wheel. Good thing I put on the lights and sirens so everyone walking along the street could see – and I didn't choose the soothing up and down wail. No, I chose the high-pitched screech that sounds like a baby screaming in your inner ear from a mile away. I also had the "new" lights with the high-intensity strobe pack; the strobes were so freaking bright that the glare and flash at night would give aliens in orbit a seizure. So there I was, driving down a residential street fish-tailing back and forth resembling an upstream salmon, with sirens wailing and lights pumping madly like a rolling, rave disco. I was about to lose control of the car with everyone watching. To top it off, the whole street was lined with parked cars on both sides. I was sure I was about to be famous in Yorktown; I was going to be the new Mountie that wiped out six cars in one accident.

As my fanny puckered I remembered my academy driver training. My instructor in one of his rare "inside voice" moments said, "When the back end starts to fishtail put the old Crown Vic's transmission in neutral. This will restore traction for the light, rear ended cars." So I put the car in neutral. Unfortunately this combined with the patchy ice and me correcting the steering only caused the car to spin one hundred and eighty degrees, so now I was going down the street backwards lights ablaze, sirens a-screech; at least ten people on the sidewalks had stopped to watch!

I knew I was going to crash; into which car or cars was the only mystery.

My car was in reverse but not quite straight, and I was listing and still sliding to one side. And then I saw it—a blessed break in the parked cars. I saw a small space of curb where a massive tree was just a few feet from it. If

I could just turn the wheel right I could aim for the patch, mount the curb, and hit the tree. It would be a crash, but into a tree, and no one's car would be damaged, and I could perhaps hide until the staff sergeant came. Bottom line was that if I could hit this tree, no one would get hurt. To punctuate the need to act fast, my partner radioed that his suspect had crashed nearby and it was now a foot chase. Although other units were responding as well, he needed help and I was closest! So I aimed and darted the wheel and the back end went right where I wanted it! But then something odd happened. The rear tire hit the curb and held, causing the front end to slide also into the curb. The car then stopped, still running in neutral, resting on the road right up against the curb. It didn't hop up the curb to the lawn as planned. So essentially, to the onlooker, and there were several, I came flying down the street in a wailing, strobe light, spaz-machine, spun the car one hundred and eighty degrees in a wicked J turn, continued in reverse, and then parallel parked in the only opening in the street – all pretty quickly.

I shut off the engine and got out to check for damage. I noticed that people on the opposite sidewalk were stopped, staring at me in disbelief. I heard some lady say to her husband, "You see that? They train those Mounties so well! That was amazing!" There was even some applause! After hearing that, I did what I felt was necessary; I pretended I was responding to *that* address and that my out-of-control, spin-parking was intentional. I whipped out my flashlight and ran up the sidewalk and made like I was looking for something—all while I radioed to my partner that I would be arriving on foot.

That day I learned the art of looking professional, despite the circumstances.

I saw an opening between houses and charged through the yard and back alley with purpose, running to my partner's crime scene. I couldn't drive on anyway, as I was sure I damaged the police car. I managed to find my partner in great time and we got his suspect.

My stunt-parking did make me famous with the public in the coming days as rumours circulated. The mechanics found no damage to the car or tires which alleviated my concerns of the staff sergeant's wrath.

A few shifts after getting out of the penalty box for my parking stunt, I left the car on a street to attend a call. While I was out of the car the road caved in sending my car down a hill and through someone's fence and backyard! Famous status revoked. And, just like that, I was just a regular Mountie, with a good story to tell.

CONFIRMATION
Constable Veronica Fox
Richmond, British Columbia

July 19, 2005 was sunny and hot. In general terms, it was a normal summer day in the lower mainland of British Columbia. It would, however, turn out to be a very exciting day for me.

The home phone rang around 1:00 PM. I didn't recognize the number and picked it up expecting to have to tell someone that I wasn't related to Michael J. Fox (this had happened before) and that no, I didn't know his number. Instead, the stranger on the other end of the phone asked to speak to me by name.

The caller on the other end of the phone identified himself as an RCMP member. I'm sure he told me his name, but I forgot it almost as soon as I heard it. "I have good news for you . . ." he said.

I nearly dropped the phone.

The voice on the other end of the phone advised me that I had been accepted by the RCMP. He gave me my troop assignment and told me I'd be leaving for Depot in about three weeks.

I left the phone to get my day planner, calling down the hall to tell Mum the good news. We both cried with excitement. I was having a hard time believing it. It had been years of hard work. Now, after several hundred miles run, and almost as many volunteer hours logged, I was finally hearing the words I had dreamed of hearing: "Welcome to the RCMP."

I returned to the phone and the voice on the other end began giving me details on what to expect in the next few weeks and how to prepare for the upcoming six months of training. Before I hung up, Mum whispered a reminder for me to say thank you. I did. I still couldn't believe it.

It had been a long journey that had taken me from my initial application to the RCMP to the phone call I received that day. As with many other applicants to the Force, I had worked hard over the course of the several months that it took to complete the long and often challenging application process.

Getting into the RCMP was no easy task, nor should it have been. I had started my journey in June 2004. After attending an information session, I wrote the RCMP police aptitude test (RPAT). The test was comprehensive and lasted several hours. It touched on everything from math, logic and memory to English grammar and writing. I waited almost two months to receive my results via mail. Only after a confirmed pass was I able to submit my detailed and thorough application package which included some medical test results, documentation on past travel and employment, character references, and, most importantly, my test results from the physical ability requirement evaluation (PARE).

The PARE was a challenging obstacle course designed to ensure that applicants could meet the physical requirements of general duty policing. It was timed and included running up and down a flight of stairs, jumping over various obstacles, completion of a pushing and pulling task, and a controlled carry of a torso bag. This was one of my biggest challenges and required many personal hours of overall physical training.

In December 2004 and January 2005, I sat for two separate interviews with police officers. Over the next several months, while the RCMP conducted a thorough check of my background, I underwent full medical, dental, and psychological exams, obtained required certificates for typing and first aid, and retook the PARE as my old score had expired by that time.

Over the course of the entire application process, I worked full time, volunteered several hours a week at my neighbourhood community policing station, and as a member of a citizen's patrol organized by a local police detachment, participated in a sports club, and maintained a strict personal workout schedule. It had been many months of hard work. Now, a year and a month following my attendance at that first information session, I viewed the phone call I'd just received to be an indication that all that work had been worth it.

All things considered, I thought the day had turned out to be fairly fantastic. I had no idea it was about to get even better.

With only three weeks to go until I left home, and with a million things to do, I decided to head out right away to purchase some items I'd need for training. Top of the list: schedule a date with my hair stylist! Mum had some shopping to do as well so she came along.

We stopped at a drug store first. While we were purchasing a parking ticket, a young lady asked us for help with the ticket dispensing machine. We spent several minutes helping her out and, as a result, were standing in the right place at the right time for what happened next.

As we were talking, I noticed a male run past us through the parking lot. This wasn't in itself very noteworthy. However, the fact that his pants appeared to be on fire definitely was. He was a pretty tall guy—at least six feet. He was wearing a black, puffy jacket which seemed out of place considering the warm weather. From his white basketball shorts he was trailing a large plume of red smoke. We all stopped mid-sentence to watch him run past. I remember at first being confused as to what I was seeing and then suddenly having this revelation—so that's what it looks like when a bank anti-theft dye pack goes off. I realized that this guy must have just ripped off the bank around the corner!

Everything happened so fast that I had no time to verbalize to Mum what I was thinking. Before I fully took in what had happened, I grabbed my cell phone and dialled 9-1-1. Leaving Mum and the young lady there, I ran after the thief. Having grown up in the community, I was fairly familiar with the area and didn't think twice about following him into a nearby alleyway.

I was put through to an operator and told her what I had seen. I then began relaying to her the male's description, location, and direction of travel. I really felt the adrenaline pumping. I won't lie, my hands were shaking. I'd never chased a bank robber before.

The guy ran to the end of the lane and rounded the corner. I tried to keep him in sight but I had left some distance between us. As I came around the corner, I realized I'd lost him. He hadn't been running that fast. Where could he have gone?

I looked around and spotted him through the window of the fast food restaurant on the corner. He was actually seated at a table counting the money right there in the restaurant. I was like, "Really?"

As I was updating the 9-1-1 operator, he suddenly came running out of the restaurant. For a brief moment in time we came face to face. Our eyes met. Here I was wearing a bright red T-shirt that said "Canada" on it, talking on a cell. I was sure he recognized me from the parking lot and realized I was calling the police.

Perhaps this story would be more exciting if I was able to say that I dropped the phone and judo-threw the bank robber over my shoulder, holding him until the police arrived. But in that brief moment I was fully aware that I was an unarmed civilian, untrained in anything other than rudimentary self-defence. I knew enough to know that bank robbers are often armed. This one seemed particularly unpredictable. As much as I might have wanted to, I knew that I possessed neither the tools nor the training to deal with something like this.

I looked around casually and shuffled my feet as I took a few steps away from the door. The operator asked me for an update.

I spoke to the operator as nonchalantly as possible, hoping he wouldn't realize I was on the phone to the cops, "Uh…" I said. "I guess . . . Well, I'll see you on Kingsway, then . . . Yeah. Right in front of the restaurant."

Amazingly, he turned and ran across the street. I followed him at a distance and saw him approach another male who had a young kid with him. To me, it looked like the bank robber was trying to convince this second male of something. The second guy was looking skeptical.

I updated the operator. "Where are your guys?" I asked.

Just then, I heard RCMP officers shouting from the lane. "Police! Get on the ground! Do it now!"

The skeptical-looking guy immediately dove for the ground, pulling his kid down with him without further urging. Meanwhile, the bank robber just stood there. The police officers had to apply some use of force tactics that I would later learn about at Depot, to get the male to comply with their orders. In the end, he was arrested without injury.

It took a bit for the officers to sort everything out. They let the second guy and the kid go when they determined they weren't involved. After robbing the bank, the suspect had actually stopped them to ask for a ride downtown in exchange for some money that, "someone had spilled red paint on." Sure. The second guy was really, quite understanding. He said he was okay with the police detaining him and knew they were just doing their jobs. His ten-year-old son described the experience to me as, "Cool." I was inclined to agree.

I am now a few months away from celebrating my fifth anniversary with the RCMP. In my very few years on the Force, I've had many different experiences. I've felt both the excitement of arriving first on scene at a crime in progress and the emotional low of delivering news of the death of a loved one. On some shifts, I've sat in the office for hours completing seemingly endless paperwork and on others I've missed meal breaks driving all night from call to call. I've sometimes worked long, arduous hours alone on complicated files and other times felt the shift fly by all too fast while working closely with a partner or team I enjoyed and trusted.

Overall, my work as a Mountie has been both challenging and rewarding. I wouldn't trade the work for anything in the world. Doing the job that we do means being willing to take on challenges, being able to take action when needed, and often deciding to run towards trouble even if everyone else is running away. This is why what happened on that sunny, summer day in July 2005 remains one of my best, favourite, and most self-defining memories. I would later draw on this memory to help me through the many challenging months of Depot training and the early years of my career. It was a confirmation for me that I was making the right choice and a start of what I hoped to be a long, exciting, and rewarding career with the RCMP.

A JOB WELL DONE
Constable Sara Clark,
Campbell River, British Columbia

I graduated from Depot in October 2004, and my first posting was to Nanaimo Detachment in British Columbia. I was excited to start with this detachment, both because of the size and because I used to lived there. My father had been stationed there from 1984 to1990.

One quiet night, in October 2006, I was working the north end of town; it was near the end of a long and boring shift. Normally, I worked the south end where most nights there would be at least one adrenaline-pumping call to keep me awake, so being up north was exceptionally painful, especially on a weeknight in October. It was about 5:30 AM, and I had thirty minutes until the end of my shift. I decided to start heading back to the detachment on the south end of town.

Just as I made that decision, a call came over the radio regarding two motorcyclists at a gas station. The passenger had fallen off one of the bikes as they were coming into the station. The call had come in from the pump attendant who wanted us to check and make sure the passenger was okay. I was close to this gas station so I headed towards it. As I was cresting the top of a small hill two motorcycles, matching the description provided, passed me going the other way. I turned my lights on as I performed a U-turn in the middle of the road and began to follow them. I then turned my emergency lights off because the motorcycles had gained some distance on me, and I was really only going to stop them to see if they were okay. I wasn't in a hurry.

Once I had caught up and was in behind them, I noticed they weren't slowing down. They were trying to get away from me! I watched as the first motorcycle reached the T intersection just ahead and made a quick left turn. The second bike reached the intersection immediately after, but for some reason, continued straight through. He drove right into a bus stop and, fortunately for him, was knocked off the motorbike. The motorbike shot out from under him and he slid, stopping just short of the front yard of a house. The motorcycle continued on, hit the front of the house, and blew up. I slammed on my brakes at the intersection, turned on my emergency lights, picked up the car radio, and asked for fire and ambulance. As I hopped out of the car and ran towards the house, the rider got up! He ran past me and jumped onto the back of the first bike that had returned when he saw the accident. It was honestly like something out of an action movie—even the part where the bad guy miraculously falls off the bike and is able to get away. Although I considered it, I did not attempt to grab or stop the rider as I saw that the house was fully engulfed in flames and that was clearly my priority.

I radioed dispatch that the two men were heading north on the first bike. I later found out that the transmission was pointless because, in my haste to get out of the police car, I had neglected to turn on my portable radio, and all dispatch had heard from me was my first request for fire and ambulance at the corner of Dover Street and Applecross Street. No one knew why I needed them, or what was going on, but they thankfully sent them anyway.

The front room of the house was fully engulfed in flames. As I approached, I noticed that the front bay window was covered in homemade Halloween decorations. My heart sank even further thinking this is a family home with children. I came up to the door and tried to open it. It was locked, but my banging on the door prompted a resident to come and open it before I could kick it in.

I ran into the house and told her, "Everyone has to get out!" She replied, "They can't." This response took me aback, and I replied, "You don't understand, the house is on fire!" She replied, "No, they can't, they're all handicapped, they can't move."

It turns out, the lady I was speaking to was a care aide, and the house I was standing in was a group home for mentally and physically handicapped adults. This clearly wasn't the situation I thought I was running into. I asked how many residents were there and she told me there were four residents, five including her. I asked her if anyone could walk on their own, and she replied that the woman who lived downstairs could walk with the aid of a walker. I told her to go downstairs and get her out of the house first. She quickly ran down the stairs and I turned around to look for the other three who were upstairs.

There were three doors down the hall. The first was the one the motorcycle had slammed into and was engulfed in flames. I picked the second one, hoping that the front room wasn't actually a bedroom and that no one was inside. I went into the second room and turned on the light. There was a lady in the bed and an electric wheelchair in the middle of the room. The lady was awake and clearly aware something was going on, so she was trying to give me directions on how to operate her wheelchair. The chair was plugged in and the battery was charging. I did my best to move it but the wheels wouldn't budge and I couldn't get it started. I tried pressing random buttons on the wheelchair, hoping to hit some sort of magic combination, but nothing worked. I looked around for a regular wheelchair or something I could use to move her but I couldn't see anything. She was slightly overweight so I knew I wouldn't be able to move her very far by myself. I evaluated the situation and knew there were two others in the house and one possibly in the front room. I didn't want to waste time trying to learn how to operate an electric wheelchair, so I just looked at her and told her I would be back and left the room. I will never forget the look on her face when I left.

I ran down the hall into the third room and found a male in a hospital-style bed with oxygen tanks along one side and a giant oxygen mask strapped to his face. I quickly grabbed the mask and tried to pull it off his face. He was fast asleep until I accidently lost grip on the mask and it smacked against his face. His eyes shot open, which startled me. I eventually was able to break the mask away from his face, pull the bed bars down, and pull him away from the oxygen. Even with the adrenaline, his dead weight was a lot for me. As soon as I had him away from the oxygen, I returned to the hall to locate the third person.

The only room left was the front room where the bike had blown up, so I ran back to that room. The care aide was just outside the hall and had found a commode to help move the lady who was in the burning room. We both entered and she helped me get her rigid body onto the commode. At that point, I knew we didn't have much time left, so I told the care aide to get out of the house. She left and I wheeled the lady on the commode out into the hall. I am not sure what kind of physical handicap she had, but her body was straight and stiff so I had to wrap one arm around her body and push the chair with the other. I wheeled her out to the hall and looked at the front door. I could see flames curling across the top of the door frame and knew we didn't have much time left to use the door. I made a run for it. Once I got to the door frame, I hit the lip and she slide off the chair, but we were outside and had cleared the house. Fortunately, a bystander, who was watching the scene, came up to the front yard and helped me carry her to the sidewalk, a safe distance from the house.

I ran back into the house with the commode to get the man out. I knew that the other lady with the impossible wheelchair was still in her room and, as I ran by, I saw that her room was not yet affected by the flame or smoke. I knew it was more important to get him further away from the oxygen so I went to him. I tried to grab him and get him on the commode. As I was doing this, I looked down the hall and saw that the fire trucks had arrived and the firemen were running towards the house. I left the man on the floor and met the firefighters in the hall. I told them about the lady in the second room, pointed to the man on the floor, and then I left out the front door.

Once outside, I spoke to the care aide and asked where the lady with the walker was. She said she left her in the backyard. I ran around the house and found the lady wandering aimlessly and unfazed down the alley. I walked her to the front of the house and to the ambulance was, by that time, the three other people were being treated.

At this point, I was finally able to look at the house and see how bad the damage was. I could see the firefighters were fighting the fire engulfing the roof. The whole side of the house was melted and engulfed in flame. The house, thankfully, was fitted with a sprinkler system which had kept the smoke down and the fire from spreading too fast inside the residence. I stood by as the firefighters took control of the fire and the victims were taken to the hospital. I watched the firefighters stumbling out of the fire, chugging water, and worrying about the oxygen. I had just spent a good ten minutes inside the burning building, without any protective gear, and was now standing outside with singed hair and eyebrows. I probably should have had myself checked out by medical personnel, but there was too much other stuff going on to worry about it at the time. I did have a cough for days afterwards.

As I was standing around, one of the firefighters asked me what had happened. By this time I had reflected on the whole incident and came to the conclusion that I had just experienced a real-life video game. I explained to him my revelation: I watched a *Die Hard*-style explosion of a motorcycle into the front of a house, and then watched the enemy get away while I tried to save the innocent civilians in the burning building.

Once inside, every room had a different challenge to figure out. The first room was engulfed in flames and had a rigid, mentally and physically handicapped lady. The second had an overweight, handicapped lady with a complicated and inoperable wheel chair. The third room had a man who was surrounded by oxygen tanks, and was completely dead weight, while the fourth resident was wandering around the neighbourhood completely unaware as to what was going on or why she was in her night gown wandering the streets at 5:30 AM. There was smoke, flames, and a sprinkler system which made the floors slippery and soaked my uniform. After all that, I still had to try and catch the bad guy.

The firefighter thought it was pretty amusing. I recall saying, "Honestly, what are the odds of the place being full of handicapped people!" He gave me a worried look and glanced over my shoulder, I followed his gaze to the group of reporters behind me. I hoped to God none of them recorded my enthusiastic statement.

Once the fire was under control, I went to see the remains of the motorcycle. Although there wasn't much to look at but melted plastic, I was able to find a license plate and, after having our dispatch run the number through CPIC, I discovered it was stolen. All the pieces came together. They weren't planning to stop for me; they had gained a lot of distance because they were trying to get away. There were only a few blocks between us so I didn't notice that they had accelerated that much. A couple of witnesses, who happened to be out walking their dog along Applecross that morning, reported that as soon as the two bikes saw me they sped up. They estimated the speed to be seventy to eighty kilometres an hour. They were curious as to why I was not trying to catch-up. Initially, I wasn't looking at them as criminals; only people I needed to ensure were okay and safe to drive. I understood why the second bike lost control. He was going too fast and was unfamiliar with the handling of that particular stolen motorcycle. At the speeds he was going, it was amazing that he was able to get up and run away.

Because of shift change and each member finishing up their work files, I didn't have much for backup during the entire call. However, I was able to get a member to locate and interview the female who had fallen off the back of the motorbike, which had initially prompted the call. She had been left at the gas station by the suspects and was still there when the member arrived. Unfortunately the interview didn't go so well. At the end of the day, we knew who one of the riders was, but we had nothing we could use for court. There was no one available to relieve me so I ended up doing scene control, and assisting the fire inspector until 2:00 PM, at which time the scene was finally cleared. I went home exhausted, had a long, hot shower, slept for about two hours, and then went back to work at 6:00 PM to start my night shift.

When I got to work, a few people asked if I had a suspect, but otherwise no one mentioned a thing about what happened. No one asked any other questions. I just grabbed my duty bag and began taking calls like on any regular shift. Three years later, I received a letter which invited me to Government House in Victoria, British Columbia to receive a Medal of Valour from the province for my part in this incident.

That was my first "job well done" and it was nice to receive it.

Editor's note: Sara is the daughter of Rick Bigland, author of the story "Summer of '77".

A SAFE RIDE HOME
Staff Sergeant Peter McTiernan
Burnaby, British Columbia

In Windsor, Nova Scotia, there are three units: the municipal unit that deals with the town of Windsor; Highway Patrol; and the Windsor Rural Detachment. The rural detachment covers a large geographical area called Hants County. The county was well-known for "the Shore" area, and its rough and tumble community dances and events. So, on this night, it was no surprise when my partner and I overheard on the police radio that members in the Shore were responding to a "shots fired" call which involved a person known to us to be violent. Being keen to assist, we acknowledged the call, activated our emergency equipment, and sped towards the Shore. We knew we were a considerable distance away, and it would take a good half hour to get there, and that was if we pushed it. While en route, our usually reliable Chevrolet police car started to smoke and make strange noises. Not long after that the car gave up entirely, right on the highway; it might have had something to do with my foot being pressed to the floor and speeding down the highway like a bat-out-of-hell.

Being completely frustrated by leaving our members to deal with the gun call, we decided to commandeer a vehicle. While waiting for a car to come along, we received word that the suspect had been taken into custody and everything was fine. So we got comfortable and waited for the towing company to show up. Of course, this involved getting the tow truck operator out of bed, and him driving a half hour to our location, it would be a minimum of an hour wait!

The battery in the car would still activate the emergency lights we so decided we would stop the next car that came along and see if we could get a ride back to the detachment. The tow truck driver could pick up the police car without us and we could get back in service. At that time in

Windsor, on a cold, October night, there was very little traffic, particularly at 1:30 AM, so we were on the side of the road for a while before the first car came along. We were pleased that we would soon be out of the cold and on our way back to the detachment. We activated the emergency lights and waived the car over to find it was occupied by four nuns on their way back from a church bingo in Halifax. That sounds like the beginning of a bad joke, but that's what happened. The good sisters, feeling charitable towards two cold Mounties working a cold night, offered us some food which we graciously declined. Since there wasn't any room in the car we waived the car on and waited for another.

Eventually another vehicle came along and again we activated the emergency equipment and waived it over. A young male was driving, and we immediately noticed the usual signs of impairment. We brought him back to the police car and had him blow into a roadside screening device (used to screen drivers who may have been drinking) which confirmed our suspicions that he was indeed impaired. We followed up with the usual cautions and the demand for him to take the Breathalyzer test (a device that measures the level of alcohol in the breath, and, therefore, blood). The suspect agreed to take the test which was back at the Windsor Detachment, a half hour drive away—when you have a car.

Legally, the test had to be administered within two hours of when we found the suspect driving. We were at risk of not getting him back in time as we had to wait for, what was at that time, two tow trucks.

My partner, who was always a resourceful and colourful member, asked the suspect what he wanted done with his car. My partner, always the thoughtful one, told the suspect that one of us could drive it back to the office and he could leave it in our detachment parking lot until either he was sober enough to drive or someone else came to pick it up. The other option, and usual practice, would be to seize his car and have the tow company hold it until he was released. He would then have to pay almost a hundred dollars in fees to get it back.

Of course, the kid agreed to the first option, and was extremely thankful that we were that considerate, and would go to such lengths to save him money. He lived in Windsor, so this really helped him.

My partner was giving me hand signals, out of sight of the suspect, and I immediately realized what he was up to and I started to laugh. He directed the suspect to his car and told him to get in the back. This was no easy feat as the car was a small two door. We threw all our equipment in the back seat and trunk of the small car and my partner got in the driver's seat. I secured the police car and then got in the passenger side of the suspect's car. Imagine the look on the suspect's face as two police officers squeezed into his small car with him! But he didn't say a word. He kept looking back at the darkened police car parked on the side of the road, but at no point did he ever ask why we were leaving our car. He just kept looking back to the car and then to us. We never told him the car was disabled; the look on his face was priceless.

Seeing that the suspect had a cassette player my partner immediately popped in a tape. Not liking the music, he asked the kid where he could find an AC/DC tape. So there we were driving with a suspect in the back of his own car, playing his music (our choice) while taking him to face impaired driving charges.

We thought we were getting confused looks from the suspect, but our co-workers at the detachment were more than a little curious when we rolled up. Once we told them what had happened, they erupted in laughter.

Even after all this, the suspect never asked why we left a seemingly good police car on the side of the road just to bring his car to the detachment. We could only imagine how his call to his lawyer went:

"I was driving home and got stopped by the cops. I only had two beers," (everyone only has two beers) "and they took me in for a Breathalyzer test which I failed, and they locked me up for the night. But the strange thing was, the cops offered to drive my car to their office so I wouldn't have to pay the tow charges. They left their police car on the side of the highway at 1:30 in the morning, and drove all three of us in my car to their office. They even asked to play my AC/DC on the way to jail."

The lawyer's response must have been, "Plead guilty!"

All in all, we were pretty proud of ourselves. We had picked up a dangerous impaired driver and were able to get ourselves back into service. The suspect who unwittingly provided us a ride back to the office was able to avoid costly impound fees.

TRAFFIC TRAGEDY
Constable Kevin Morris
Chilliwack, British Columbia

What I remember most about the scene, the part that sticks in my mind, and replays anytime I pass where it happened, is the smell of the burning car. I think it was a Ford Thunderbird, but upon arrival at the accident, I couldn't really tell right away. I also remember thinking, "Bodies, yes, those are bodies strewn on the ground. People aren't supposed to be thrown around like that, it looks unnatural." I remember thinking, "It isn't supposed to be like this."

I have seen dead people before. And, I have certainly seen my share of destroyed cars, having even wrecked one or two in my time. In the RCMP there are two types of people: Mounties who have wrecked a car and Mounties who will—it's just part of the job. You just never know when it's going to happen. You'll notice that police officers almost always wear their seat belts. Seat belts… I remember one of the firefighters cursing under his breath, "They should have been wearing seat belts."

My first posting was Surrey, British Columbia. The lower mainland in British Columbia is the RCMP action and adventure capital of Canada. We get it all! With the concentration of people flocking to the warmer winters and stunning summers here in B.C., and the proximity to Vancouver, there is a real mix of people in Surrey. And of course, with any population, eighty percent of the problems are caused by twenty percent of the people. Those twenty percent keep us busy. For a first posting, Surrey was the place to be. I've chased stolen cars, been in foot chases with armed suspects, and backed-up the dog- man; it seemed like it would be action and adventure all the time. Chasing bad guys every night, it was hard to believe that they paid me to do this!

My job was called "general duty" or often simply GD. GD is the backbone of the RCMP. Across the country, GD members are the front line. In Surrey it means you're the street cop; you answer radio calls, drive a marked car, and work in uniform. Our operation is large enough that we're broken into shifts called a "watch". And as a team, we'd hit the streets and deal with anything that happens.

It was just before 2:00 AM. I remember this because when I got the call, I had my cruiser tucked in near the bar waiting for problems to arise. As I sat in my police car monitoring the front of the watering hole, I heard a series of toned broadcasts over the police radio. I knew this to be a tone to alert members of a priority call coming in. Often police communications are like that broken-telephone game where between the caller and the cop, things are reported differently than they actually happened. Our dispatchers are great: we get information over the radio and over the computer, but if they are getting inaccurate information that is what they pass on. That is how a dog bite call is actually a barking dog complaint, and sometimes an armed robbery call is actually a kid shoplifting. Sometimes when you get a call, you hope it is a broken- telephone call, you hope that five dead on scene actually means five injured. But most of the time, including this time, the dispatchers have it spot on.

I knew time was not on my side. I activated my emergency lights and siren and raced off to the scene of the accident, knowing that people were in trouble and needed help. I was one of the first police cars there. I remember there was a fire truck already on scene, and I remember the sight… in fact it replays in slow motion in my head as I write this sentence. I pulled my police car up to the scene blocking the travel portion of the roadway. Ahead of me I saw nothing but pure destruction. To my left, I saw firefighters working hard to put out a fire in a ditch, on the road ahead of me I saw three pieces of what appeared to be a car. And then of course, there were the victims of the accident, all of them had been ejected from the vehicle. I also did not realize that it was a car in the ditch that firefighters were working on putting out.

I remember the smell and I remember flashes of conversations at the scene. The firefighter talking about seatbelts, another Mountie was on the radio asking if there was a police dog available to look for any other persons who may have been ejected from the vehicle. There were fields on both sides of the road and a body, or body part in this case, could have been flung out of sight into the field. The totality of the scene was really overwhelming. It felt like I was taking in all the disaster for an hour, but it was really only a couple of minutes in real time. The ambulance was just arriving, another officer was handling the coordination of the fire and ambulance traffic, I grabbed my gear and went to close the road. As I passed the second car, I looked in and will never forget the heartbreaking sight of the teenaged life lost inside the burnt-out car.

Imagine a cop, bulletproof vest, Batman belt with all the tools, a uniform, sturdy issued boots, fully prepared. The cop in your mind is well trained, having gone through six months of training at Depot and having gone through another six months of field coaching on the street. This is the person you'd want to restore order in an emergency; this is the person you'd want to help if were in distress. Now picture that cop's face; put your face on that image. Fill the uniform like it is a shell with all of your insecurities and apprehensions, but don't forget to fill it with your experiences and your courage too. Now picture yourself getting out of the police car that night. There is a car burning and bodies on the pavement. There really is no difference between me and anyone else. Sure I have some training, but I'm also human. It was really the smell that made it real. I remember thinking, "What could I have done to prevent this?" and "What do I need to do now?"

Flashback… I remember a paramedic bending down next to a body lying in the middle of the roadway, checking his vital signs for what seemed like a minute or two, and then saying "This one's gone," and moving on to the next victim. To be honest, the next thing I remember is another police officer asking me to move my police vehicle to an intersection approximately a kilometre up the roadway to divert traffic away from the accident scene.

At the time, being one of the junior members on scene, I was looking to the more experienced members, whom I thought had dealt with these sorts of things on a regular basis, to tell me what to do. I thought that these types of things were a common occurrence, accidents happen all the time, and I assumed that my co-workers had been to scenes like this one before. It wasn't until months later that I realized that this was unlike any other file I would experience in my career.

Now you have to understand that at the time I was only twenty-three years old. This accident was the most serious, most horrifying, and tragic thing I had ever encountered. Five people dead, five people that had done nothing wrong. They had family and friends, just like I did. They were just hanging out, living life, and in less than fifteen seconds, they were all dead, and for what?

There would be five early-morning door knocks that would change those families' lives forever. Although it was my job and I was required to do it, I was just hoping it wasn't me that had to walk from my police car up to the front door of those houses and let those families know that their son, their brother, their family member, was dead.

Sitting blocking traffic on the roadway for at least five hours, I really got to thinking. I started to realize the devastation, the carnage, and the emotional heartbreak of the situation that was not only going to affect me, but dozens of friends and family members of the victims.

They say whatever doesn't kill you makes you stronger. This may be true. But there are a few steps between an incident and being stronger for it. It is hard for me to put all this into words. Those families lost their kids. It seems almost petty for me to be talking about; how it all affected me when I didn't lose anything. My heart goes out to those families, it really does. I guess I just want to recognize the bigger picture, and note that I am just one story in the bigger picture, that is all.

Six in the morning came really quickly as I sat in my car reliving all of the things that I had just experienced. It was finally time for day shift to take over my position blocking traffic. It was hard to believe that four hours later the road was still closed. Now from where I was, I couldn't see what investigation was being conducted or completed. I only remember when the coroner showed up in a white van, just as the sun was coming up. It struck me; the day for many people was just starting, but not for those people, they would be leaving in that stark-white van.

When I got home that morning, I was filled with different emotions and feelings that I had not felt before: hopelessness, sorrow, and despair, just to name a few. I was taking personal responsibility for the accident. I was nowhere near the accident when it happened, never met any of the kids, and I had never seen the cars before, but I was running scenarios in my head where I could have prevented the accident. I guess I was trying to rewrite what happened in my head so I could believe it didn't happen.

One of the key roles for police officers has always been to restore order. Chaos happens. We swoop in with our lights, uniforms, and unmovable intent, and restore order. People need that. Humpty fell off the wall and if we can't put Humpty back together again we take Humpty away and clean up the mess. The accident was cleaned up. All those details to make the public feel better were in place, and to drive by the scene now, you wouldn't know what happened there. The general public as a whole had moved on. I was left with a lot of questions. I was having trouble restoring order within myself. How do you reconcile such a tragedy?

The first couple of days after the accident were the hardest for me. I came home that morning and just lay wide awake in bed. My wife was a huge comfort then. For a while after the accident, I had a hard time sleeping and being at work was difficult. Even now, I get a flood of reaction from being back at the spot where it happened, even if I am just travelling through.

To say there is a silver lining in something like this is abhorrent. The loss was catastrophic for the families, and put me under great strain. Through the healing powers of time and the friendship of my amazing wife Kelly, I was able to come to some conclusions and take away some learning from my experience.

I have come to believe things happen for a reason. I can't tell you the reason why this happened; I just have faith that there was a larger plan at work. The reason isn't for me to worry about all the time. And moving forward, I have dealt with other tragedies, both mine personally in the loss of a close friend in a motor vehicle accident, and in the tragedies we're called to deal with in the RCMP. The faith that I found in my belief of "things happening for a reason" philosophy has served me well. I still feel the loss in tragedies. I want to feel this; I take pride in my empathy. But I function better. I guess once you have been there, the second, third, and fourth times are understood better. It happens for a reason. Also, although the accident was a key defining moment in my very junior career, a point that I will never forget, it isn't the only memorable event of my policing career. There are events that I take great pride in: helping people with their relationships, directly helping a kid onto the right path, and, even since that tragic evening, I have saved a person's life. These are the reasons that I love being a Mountie.

Sometimes, in this job, I am overcome with sadness and sorrow, but most times I am overcome with pride with the work I get to do.

HOPE COLLIDES
Constable April Dequanne
Toronto, Ontario

It's Wednesday, 7:00 AM and the sergeant calls the team in for a meeting. "We have a new lead on Jamal, but we need to move in quickly." Jamal was a name that I recognized; we have been trying to locate him for weeks with little success. He was wanted on an immigration warrant for removal from Canada for serious criminal offences committed here in Canada. "We have Intel that he is armed and dangerous, and is only visiting his 'baby mom' over the next two days," the sergeant states. "And once we have visual, we'll get a warrant to gain access to the apartment and arrest him." The sergeant went on to explain that Jamal is six feet tall, two-hundred and thirty pounds, and has a lengthy criminal record, including drugs and weapons charges—we should be vigilant.

It's Tuesday, 3:00 PM, I've locked my guns and handcuffs away for the day and I've removed by soft body armor and replaced it with a T-shirt that says "COACH" across the back. I was on my way to the Running and Reading Club at a middle school in Thistle Town, a tough neighbourhood in Toronto. Every Tuesday during the school year, I have the privilege of mentoring kids on how to achieve their goals through fitness and literacy. Our hope is to shorten the gap between the "haves" and "have nots". It's a duty I feel just as strongly about as being a member of the RCMP. The kids have come to know me as "Coach April" and do not know that I am a police officer. The police/community relations are not at its best in Thistle town, and I prefer the kids know me as Coach April and not "Police Officer April".

Wednesday, 8:03AM, and I'm sitting in my van in the apartment parking lot of our target. I see kids exiting the building by the dozen, some with

- 142 -

parents, some without, and some with backpacks and lunch bags, some without. I think to myself, "No way would I let my child walk to and from school alone." Just last week there was a shooting in the community centre next to the school and a CRIPS versus BLOOD gang war was raging. As kids filed past my van, I slumped low in my seat and gave a silent prayer that the kids would not see me. We were working uncomfortably close to my Running and Reading school.

Tuesday, 4:08 PM: "Coach April, can you help me tie my shoes?" asked Benjamin. "Sure little buddy, then you can show me how fast you can run." I bent over and tied-up his shoes. Benjamin's shoes appeared far too big for his feet, and were well worn, with the soles beginning to peel off at the ends, but Benjamin seemed to float effortlessly across the gym floor with them securely tied on.

Wednesday, 8:18 AM: we're lined up outside the apartment door, weapons drawn, and ready to make our entry. We believed Jamal was inside along with his "baby mom" and whoever else may be inside the apartment. We had been watching the apartment since our early arrival and there seemed to be no movement inside and nobody had come or gone. We approach quietly, I could hear my heart pounding, and I could hear the quiet breathes of a teammate behind me. A teammate approaches the front of the door carrying the fifty pound metal door ram (what we affectionately call the "Master Key to the City"). Our Master Key was poised and ready for use.

Back to Tuesday, 4:36 PM: "When you're waiting for something good to happen to you." That was the definition of "hope" given to us by one of our R&R kids. Each week we introduce a new character building word; you see, the Running and Reading Club is not just about running and reading. We also provide a social-development-rich environment so that when things get tough for kids, they have an arsenal of character attributes to draw from for personal protection and resilience.

Back to Wednesday, 8:23 AM: Like slow motion, I see the door ram swing like a giant wrecking ball on a crane, the door shakes, the door frame cracks, and the deadbolt lock ricochets into the air. "POLICE!" The silence broken, I no longer heard the pounding of my heart or the breathing. We all made our presence known, and once inside the apartment we quickly realize that there are more people inside than our initial projections.

Tuesday, 4:42 PM: I'm reading from the book, *Terry Fox, A Story of Hope*. Sixty kids who have run out of energy are sitting quietly, hanging on every word I read. Sixty pairs of eyes and ears were looking to hear about "hope" from Coach April.

Wednesday, 8:24 AM: We know who Jamal is and what threat he poses, but we don't know who the other three adults in the apartment are. Immediately the need to secure everyone is paramount to our safety. Unfortunately the individuals inside the apartment don't understand that need and the fight is on.

Tuesday, 4:44 PM: "Coach April, how come Terry never gave up?" A little voice from the back of the room enquires.

"Because Terry was very brave," I respond.

Wednesday, 8:25 AM: I've wrestled Jamal to the ground and a teammate is positioned to put the handcuffs on him when I get a tap on the shoulder. I can hear my heart pounding, I can hear the breathing and in slow motion, I turn not knowing the threat, ready to strike, and it is like I'm hit! A feeling of nausea fills my being; I shake my head as if the blinding would go away.

Tuesday, 4:58 PM: Cleanup is done and we're preparing to send the kids on their way home. "Remember to practice hope this week and be brave like Terry, because sometimes hope is found in the brave things we do." The kids, tired from the hour of running, their minds filled with a story, and hearts filled with hope, exit in a mad rush.

Wednesday 8:27 AM: "Coach April"... I'm hit again, blind-sided, not with a fist or some inanimate object, but with a set of big brown eyes, filled with hope. I jump up and grab Benjamin to remove him from the living room, hoping to protect him from seeing what is about to happen to his father, Jamal.

Thursday 7:30 AM, in the office boardroom, I'm quiet in the debriefing of yesterday's arrest of Jamal. Gripped with the sorrow I feel for Benjamin, I don't have the energy to add to the conversation. Distracted, I sit silently with the hope that Benjamin understood that on Tuesday I'm "Coach April" and Wednesday I was "Police Officer April" and on both days, I'm just trying to provide hope.

Be brave Benjamin, be brave!

SAFETY BEAR ATTACKS
Staff Sergeant Tony Gollob
Bowmanville, Ontario

Tony Gollob was working at the Toronto International Airport Detachment, which at the time had over four hundred and sixty members, and was the largest detachment in the country. With only a couple of years on the Force, he was quite junior. Junior members were often requested to participate in public or community events. This event would be a high-profile community relations event at the airport in support of Police Week. The most recognizable police uniform, possibly worldwide, is the RCMP's scarlet riding garb known as the Red Serge. All Mounties have Red Serge stories: whether it's having our photos taken with celebrities, comments made by the public when they see us in our formal attire, or even stories where the Mountie in Red Serge gets into a foot chase and has to tackle a criminal. These stories are always told with pride as they are unique to us.

In the early years, especially, it was expected that Mounties make public appearances. Unfortunately for Tony, the event he was assigned to didn't require him to wear the Red Serge.

"Safety Bear?" Tony asked.

"You get four hours off for being the Safety Bear for a couple of hours work on shift, it's a good deal!" his supervisor replied.

Safety Bear is the RCMP mascot. To be fair, the oversized, plush bear is wearing a Red Serge, and in fact it was a temporary promotion as Safety Bear wears the rank of a sergeant.

This was of little consolation to Tony, as the costume had the odour of an entire hockey team! It must have been used in the middle of summer and put away soaking wet. Soaking wet with someone else's sweat. Tony tried not to think about that.

The costume includes the body, a pair of furry, three-fingered mitts, and the head. Tony, with help, climbed into the body and positioned the feet so he could walk, fastened the Velcro connectors to the gloves, and his helpers positioned the head on Tony to complete the costume.

The head on the costume required Tony to look out a small opening in the mouth. There was a small fan positioned in the headpiece to help keep him cool, but it wasn't working. It likely shorted out due to the copious sweat of previous Safety Bear victims.

The plan was to have Safety Bear interact with the public and let people pose with Safety Bear for Polaroid pictures that they would be able to keep as a souvenir.

Constable Jeanne Balaban brought the detachment's Polaroid and helped Tony, aka Safety Bear, into the van, and they headed for Terminal One to interact with the public. Jeanne was also in costume; she was wearing a tuxedo.

Inside the terminal Jeanne realized that she forgot the film. She left Safety Bear by himself just outside one of the screening points.

This delay gave Tony the opportunity to reflect on just how uncomfortable he was. Sweat was already dripping down his back, and with every breath he had to concentrate on not gagging; the smell was so bad he could taste it.

Standing there, trying to see out the mouth of the costume, Tony heard an adult say, with a heavy Newfie accent, "Hey look at the moose!"

"A moose?" Tony said to himself, "I'm a bear."

To see who could possibly think he was moose, Tony turned just in time to see a fist flying towards him! The fist belonged to a drunk, moose-hating Newfie, and he connected with the oversized head, spinning it ninety degrees, blinding Tony except for a small dot of light he could see through his peripheral vision.

Not knowing what else to do, he dove in the last known direction of the assailant. He got him! And the fight was on. The Newfie was swinging as hard as he could, but couldn't hurt Tony through the costume, and Tony couldn't control the Newfie or land any useful strikes on him because of his cartoon-like hands.

Jeanne came around the corner and saw Safety Bear rolling around with the drunk. She put in the "Safety Bear in need of assistance" call on her radio, and in short order, Jeanne and several other laughing Mounties separated the two. The drunk was arrested for at least assault, and possibly cruelty to animals.

Now Tony was really uncomfortable. The question for Tony in the suit was which part of his body was the least soaked in sweat? And, he had just gotten into a fight and was still seeing red. The string of jokes from his co-workers probably didn't help.

Jeanne suggested that they go to Terminal Two and meet some of the kids on the outgoing Jamaica flight. So, they packed-up into the van and took the short ride over to T-2.

Things started okay. Safety Bear was patting kids' heads, giving hugs, and high-fives, and everyone was friendly. One would think that attacking a six foot and four inch tall bear wouldn't be the first thought on a child's mind, but, unprovoked, a little snot walked up and kicked Safety Bear in the shin.

"We need to be nice to Safety Bear," said Jeanne, putting herself between the kid and Tony. Tony tried to walk away with Jeanne providing a tactical block. This is called "tactical repositioning" and is usually used when facing a lethal threat, but you do what comes naturally.

Kids are pack animals. Sensing weakness, and that Tony and Jeanne were separated, they attacked as a group! They were pulling on the fur, grabbing legs, and trying to climb Safety Bear! Tony, entirely under siege, started to swat kids off of him like an ogre fending off villagers.

Between the two, they were able to quell the "children of the corn" and Tony decided that enough was enough and it was time to go.

Exhausted and soaked in sweat, Tony followed Jeanne towards the exit. Just before they left, a pair of attractive airline stewardesses asked if they could have a picture with Safety Bear. "Maybe things are improving," Tony thought.

He stood in the middle of the two stewardesses and Jeanne positioned the camera. But due to the number of shots taken that day, the camera was taking a little while to charge the flash.

To pass the time, the stewardesses were playfully rubbing Safety Bear's belly. Actually, one was scratching more than rubbing! Tony is a tall guy, and the Safety Bear costume rides low. The belly of the costume, on Tony, sat right over his groin. He was being assaulted in a whole new way!

Jeanne was still waiting for the flash to charge when Tony called out, "Jeanne! Just take the picture!"

All is well that ends well though, Tony did survive. He decided to focus on his policing career and leave the mascot work to the professionals. To this day though, Tony reports an affinity for sports highlight reels where the mascots are fighting. He's been there.

THE WIDOW MAKER
Corporal Robert Gaetz (Ret.)
Whitehorse, Yukon

It was a mild, summer's evening on Victoria Island. My partner Randy and I were in Sidney, British Columbia having a cup of joe with the night watchman at the Sidney Hotel at about three in the morning. The Sidney Hotel was on the waterfront, overlooking the Strait of Georgia, the Gulf Islands, and Mount Baker in the distance. Suffice it to say, it was a relaxing moment on the graveyard shift that night. Then we got a call from Colwood Operational Communication Centre (our dispatchers). There was a "break and enter in progress" at the Ready Chef Restaurant; it was reported by a neighbour who could see lights on and movement inside the restaurant. We bailed outta there and were on our way.

The Ready Chef Restaurant was a little burger joint just a half block off Beacon Avenue in Sidney. It was separated by a two-metre-wide alley between it and a dry cleaner on the other side. I was the first to arrive. I parked my car about one door up the street and ran down the alley to the back of the restaurant. I could see that the back door was wide open and an interior light was on and shining out the doorway. I got on my portable radio to advise Randy of what I had found. While I was doing so, Sonny came out the back door with his arms full of milk and cookies. I recognized him on sight; I had arrested Sonny before and he was well-known to the local RCMP.

Upon seeing me, Sonny gave me a deer in the headlights look, and then turned and ran down the alley away from me toward the street. He clearly wasn't thinking straight because while he was running he was still trying to carry all the milk and cookies. This had the effect of slowing him down while some of his haul was falling as he tried to run. I gave chase and, as we approached the street, Sonny was cut off by Randy who arrived on the scene in his police car. Sonny turned left and ran up the sidewalk and we continued to chase. He ran about fifteen to twenty metres up the sidewalk and into a grocery store parking lot. I got close enough to give him a shove between the shoulder blades and set him off balance. This caused him to put his arms out and he dropped the rest of his milk and cookies. Then Sonny decided to do something really stupid. He spun around and he put up his dukes, just like an old-school boxer.

Now, Sonny was a little wiry guy, about forty-five-years-old, and likely weighed in at about ninety-eight pounds soaking wet. He had long black hair, a Fu-Manchu moustache, and an unshaven face. His health had long since deteriorated due to too many years of hard drug and alcohol abuse. Randy and I were both in our mid twenties; we both weighed in at two hundred-plus pounds, probably closer to two hundred and twenty pounds with all the police gear on. We were both about five years out of training and in decent physical condition.

Keep in mind also, this was before expandable batons, pepper spray or conducted energy weapons (tasers). You might have had a nightstick and your handcuffs. Back then, we dealt with things pretty hands-on. In this case, neither of us were carrying anything other than the basic issue (cuffs, a six shot revolver, and speed loaders for the revolver). When Sonny spun around and postured to fight, he stopped dead in his tracks, and by doing so, he effectively made my decision for me, as I really didn't have time to think about it. All I wanted to do was stop the chase, make the apprehension, and prevent him from punching me in the process. So, in that fraction of a second that I had to think about it, I figured tackling him would be the most effective way to accomplish all that.

The moment Sonny spun around to put up his dukes, I was about half a step behind him and running flat out to catch him. Unbeknownst to me, Randy was about half a step behind me. Sonny didn't stand a chance. We tackled him like a couple of linebackers taking out the quarterback, with twice the force that Sonny probably thought possible. Even after such a hard hit, Sonny continued to struggle, but we had little difficulty in flipping him over onto his stomach, and then pinning him to the ground by kneeling on him. Then Sonny held his arms close to his chest to prevent them from being handcuffed. It was a fairly simple matter to pry out his arms, one at a time, and handcuff him behind his back. After taking a breath, Randy and I got up off him, and I grabbed him by the shirt collar and belt to pick him up off the ground.

As I picked him up, I saw there was a gun right under his belly, right where his hands were! Holy Crap! He had a gun!

Or that is how it appeared. In fact, it was Randy's gun and it had come out of its holster during the scuffle. Sonny had no idea that he was laying on the revolver when we were handcuffing him.

The "Sam Browne" belt we were using at the time had a full coverage leather holster. This holster can still be seen as part of any member's Red Serge uniform. It had a full leather flap covering the revolver, which was secured by either a metal peg with a hole in the flap or with a snap. With continued use, the hole in the flap of this holster became too soft to grip the peg and the flap would come open. Members were constantly dropping their guns! The most common gun drop would be on the floor of the police car right under the driver's seat, as it would come out as you were getting in or out of the car.

The Force tried to solve the problem by putting a snap on the holster to keep the flap shut. However, this caused as many problems as it solved, because some snaps would open freely, but some wouldn't and that was a problem when you needed your gun. Some members referred to this holster as the "widow maker" and as to whether it ever made a widow or not, I'm not sure, but nobody liked using it. It came close that night. The problem was finally solved in the early 1990s when the RCMP renovated the working uniform and adopted the grey shirt and the "Sam Black" gun belt and holster. On this occasion after seeing what happened to Randy's gun I immediately checked my holster and thankfully, my gun was still there, but the flap was open.

Randy recovered his revolver and we secured Sonny in the back of Randy's police car. We gathered the dropped milk and cookies and we returned to the scene of the crime to see if anything else was missing. Sonny must have had the late night growlies, because all he took was food from the kitchen.

After a few minutes Randy went back to his car to take Sonny to the office and book him into cells. I stayed behind to meet with the restaurant owner, and about a half hour later I joined Randy back at the office. When I looked in on Sonny in the cellblock, I noticed that he was wearing a pair of RCMP overalls and that his clothing was all wet and hanging on the outer door of the cellblock. I asked Randy what happened. He related that he had to help Sonny clean himself up after bringing him back to the office. Randy explained that when he got back into his police car, he could smell a foul odour inside the car. When he asked what the smell was, a teary-eyed Sonny replied, "You guys hit me so hard, I shit my pants."

THIS ONE'S FOR YOU
Sergeant Roger Waite
Halifax, Nova Scotia

R oger Waite, in the early 1990s, was working in a CPIC Operations Unit supporting Nova Scotia and Prince Edward Island. His job was to help CPIC (Canadian Police Information Centre: a computer system that is the central hub to criminal indexing, but can also be used to find lost items, stolen cars, etc.) with training, audits, breach investigations, and access requests. He had some work to do out at the Springhill Federal Institute; it was a nice day for a drive in eastern Canada so he struck out through the Wentworth Valley in an unmarked, non-descriptive, Chevy Corsica.

Driving an unmarked police car allows Mounties to be up close to all sorts of offences—imagine the traffic offences they see in any given hour. Most of the time, an unmarked car is selected because the Mountie wants to get from point A to point B with as little fuss as possible. Sometimes it is because of operational reasons where advertising police presence isn't helpful or, as in this case, the task is administrative.

Most traffic offences observed while in an unmarked unit are tolerated, meaning that, unless the driver's actions are likely to cause immediate or future damage or injury, they are not pulled over. There are plenty of marked units and uniformed Mounties out there to handle the failing to signal a lane change or minor speeding infractions.

Sometimes, someone identifies himself as "needing to talk to the police". You have all seen them out there: the driver who is so rude and self-absorbed that they have no business travelling on a public roadway.

As Roger was taking his relaxing cruise on his way to Springhill, traffic started to naturally slow during one section of the drive and there was a small backup of cars. He noticed that there was a car at the back of the pack swerving back and forth and driving very close to the car in front of it.

Roger was curious as to how this action would get the traffic moving faster or get the driver to his destination more quickly.

Eventually they all made it to a passing lane. All were able to get around the slower vehicles and get back into the lane. The car at the back pulled out and passed several cars at once and took the time to give Roger the "signal". By "signal" we mean the one finger salute, the Trudeau finger, the driver thought Roger was number one or sometimes known as the flipping of the bird.

Roger, being an alert Mountie, noticed that he was the only recipient of the "signal" despite there being a long line of cars. As Roger chuckled to himself, he came to the conclusion that the "signal" must have been a request for assistance of some kind and he'd better pull the poor lad over to see if there was a problem.

Roger dug around under the seat and found the only piece of police equipment in the old car, a rotating red light, known as a "fireball". The vehicle had no radio and it was a little early yet for widespread cellphone usage. Roger didn't even have a ticket book. Reminiscent of a *Starsky and Hutch* episode, Roger threw the fireball on the roof and revved his under-powered and under-equipped CPIC car to close the distance on the lad who had waved the distress signal.

With the car pulled over, Roger waited a few seconds in his car to let all the other motorists in the convoy pass, allowing for a safe approach to the offending car, but also so Roger could see the satisfaction of the other motorists seeing the aggressive car pulled over.

Good police officers know their authorities under law. Typically, in any given situation, there is a selection of enforcement options. But here, there was clearly a problem that needed to be addressed, but Roger's options were limited. With no ticket book, he'd have to find the kid again to issue a ticket, plus, bird-flipping isn't specifically covered in the Motor Vehicle Act of Nova Scotia. Without a radio in the car, checking warrants or insurance or a driving record was impossible.

Roger approached the car and identified himself with his Mountie badge. The driver was in his early twenties.

"Good morning. Corporal Waite, RCMP," started Roger. "How can I help you?"

This was met with a perplexed look by the driver.

"What do you want?" Roger finished.

"Ah, sorry sir, I don't understand," said the driver.

"You *waved* me over didn't you? That was a wave you gave me wasn't it?" said Roger. There was a jump in the driver's Adam's apple and shifting in his seat and his face flushed a little.

"Ah, ah, ah," he murmured.

"License and permit please," said Roger. The kid handed over the documents and Roger headed back to his car. Without a radio, there was nothing to do in the car, so he thought for a few moments about the situation.

It clicked for Roger. The look of the kid, the awkwardness, the immediate use of the word "sir" to address him, it was a good bet that the kid was an RCMP applicant. In that case, it was worth having a little fun, and if he was an applicant, there would have to be some significant changes in attitude and driving habits to be a police officer.

Back at the window of the car Roger said, "A lot of cars on the road today."

"Yes sir," he said, cementing Roger's belief that the kid was an RCMP applicant.

"I imagine you passed some along the way?" asked Roger.

"Yes sir."

"Well, now they have passed you," Roger said.

"Yes sir."

"Where are you headed?" asked Roger.

"Moncton, New Brunswick," said the driver.

"Oh perfect! I am heading that way too. You drive off, but to be safe, let's make sure you don't lose sight of me in your rear-view, okay?" Roger said.

"Ah, yes sir."

For the next ten miles or so the kid did exactly as he was asked. He drove a little in the distance, slowing if Roger slowed, speeding a head a little if Roger sped up.

The Springhill exit is on a curve, and as the kid made the bend Roger sped up the ramp and vanished from the kid's life. Roger wonders how far the kid went before he realized Roger had dropped him or, even, if the kid drove back to find him.

Roger wonders if the kid, maybe as a police officer somewhere, tells this story as often as he does. Although not a typical enforcement option, Roger was able to do a service to all the courteous drivers out there and have a little fun at the same time. At very least the kid will think twice before being so rude to fellow motorists—a good lesson for all of us.

FULL CIRCLE
Corporal Tim Popp
North Battleford, Saskatchewan

There is a grave in Ecoivres, France where the remains of Lieutenant John Henry Storer lay, as one of the millions who died in the First World War.

There was a traffic stop in Sanford, Florida in 2008, and a small revolver was seized from the suspicious occupant of the vehicle.

Fort Battleford, Saskatchewan is now a historic site with a museum that focuses on the events on the Northwest Rebellion, where government forces and civilians made their stand against Louis Riel and his supporters. In 1966, the museum was the target of a break and enter robbery.

These three events are connected. And they connect through Corporal Tim Popp, a Mountie currently working in Battleford, Saskatchewan.

When the call came in to the Battleford Detachment about an antique revolver, it was good fate that it went to Tim. Tim is a history buff, specifically in the area of the Mounted Police who served in the Klondike Gold Rush period (1897 to1902). He is involved with several military and historical associations such as the Maple Leaf Legacy Project (www.maple-leaflegacy.ca) who track down and photograph the headstones of the one hundred and ten thousand Canadian graves abroad from the First and Second World Wars. Tim is also on the board at the local museum as a military expert and researcher. So this call, that had roots over a hundred years old, was well placed with Tim.

In the fall of 2008, The City of Sanford Police Department in Florida found a man sleeping in a car. They became suspicious of the man, as he was acting nervous while talking to the police. One thing lead to another and the man ended up getting searched. They found a small Iver Johnson, thirty-two caliber, five shot pistol, no bigger than the palm of an adult's hand. Usually when a criminal gets a hold of a gun, they obliterate the serial number in an effort to erase the history of the weapon. Fortunately with this pistol, the serial number is in a discreet location; you need to know where to look. The four digit serial number was still intact. Just four digits though, that is barely an ATM code by today's standard. The likelihood of a four digit number leading back to an owner was slim.

The Americans tried to find the owner to no avail. It would have been easy for the Florida cops to shrug their shoulders and throw the pistol into the smelter and conclude their file. But fortunately they ran the serial number on the Canadian Police Information Centre (CPIC) computer system.

Most people's experience with CPIC is the annoying criminal record search you have to do to in order to volunteer or for a job working with kids. But CPIC is way more dynamic than just that small function. Basically, CPIC is an inventory system where practically anything can be uploaded to be accessed in the future. People, such as criminals or even people who wander due to Alzheimer's, can be loaded into CPIC in with correct addresses and histories. Also, vehicles that are lost or stolen, boats, currency, bicycles—you name it, anything with a serial number or descriptor, if lost or found, can be loaded into the system and searched at a later date. Fortunately, the American police officers knew this and checked the meager four digit serial number on CPIC. There was a hit, and Tim got the call.

Let's back-up to 1885. Saskatchewan was host to what became known as the Northwest Rebellion where there were pitched battles between Metis, who are a mix of French-Canadian and First Nations peoples, and government forces. Some of the government forces were made up of the North West Mounted Police. The North West Mounted Police became the Royal North West Mounted Police who became the Royal Canadian Mounted Police, who we are today. For the record, members of any of these organizations have been known as Mounties. The Rebellion is a challenging and important piece of Canadian and RCMP history. One of the Mounties who was there was John Henry Storer.

Having been born and raised in Paisley, Ontario, Storer decided to seek a life of western adventure and joined the NWMP at the age of eighteen on April 19, 1882. The records of Library and Archives Canada show that Storer was posted at Fort Battleford, and had been involved in some of the major incidents before and during the North West Rebellion. June 1884 saw Storer accompany thirty other NWMP members into a very large native encampment to arrest a native person for assault. This became known as the "Craig Incident" in NWMP annals.

During the North West Rebellion which started in March 1885, and during the siege of Battleford, the telegraph lines were cut. To report his situation, the commander of Fort Battleford, Inspector William Morris, needed to get word to the closest point in the railway line at Swift Current. Stationed at Swift Current were Canadian Colonel William Otter and a column of government forces ready to head north to Fort Battleford. Calling on volunteers to take written dispatches to Colonel Otter, only one member stepped forward, Constable John Storer.

Constable Storer and a native guide, James Bird, left in broad daylight and travelled as fast as their mounts could carry them. It was reported that the full out chase, as the two departed Battleford, lasted for about sixty miles with potshots being taken from both sides. Reaching Swift Current, two hundred miles away in forty-eight hours, Storer delivered the dispatches and began his trip back, this time during the night and accompanied with a few other riders.

This ride brought Storer's name to the attention of the NWMP Comptroller Fred White in Ottawa. For his exploits, Storer was immediately promoted to corporal and continued to ride in scouting missions toward Cut Knife where there was an impending battle between government forces and the First Nations band. John Storer was present and fought at the Battle of Cut Knife Hill on May 2, 1885.

John Storer left the NWMP at the rank of sergeant after five years of service. In those days, initial engagement to the NWMP was five years and it was like military service; it was quite restrictive. You couldn't marry in that five years and you couldn't decide to quit. Also, you couldn't go into debt and often you couldn't live outside the detachment or local "Mountie house". In those days, members often left at the end of their five year engagement simply because they wanted to own property and get married; the pay wasn't that great either.

Storer was a businessman and contractor and became Battleford's first overseer (mayor). Eventually he lied about his age (he was too old at fifty-two) and signed up for the First World War. The military, figuring that he was perhaps on the older side of the draft, put him in a transport and supply position. In the military he held the rank of Lieutenant. But war is dangerous. He was killed in action near Vimy Ridge on March 5, 1917, one month prior to the big battle that helped forge Canada on the world stage.

Between the time that Storer left the NWMP and enlisted for service in the Great War, he had bought the five shot Iver Johnson pistol. Due to its size, it would have been bought as a personal protection weapon that could be easily slipped into a suit pocket or handbag. It was still unsettled times in western Canada, the violence of the Rebellion and the fallout of Louis Riel's and other Metis and First Nation executions were fresh on everyone's minds. Storer didn't leave the community when he resigned as a Mountie. He stayed and took a municipal roll, his past in the NWMP would have been widely known. He likely carried the weapon as a last resort for his personal protection.

John was married to Effie Storer. The couple had three children, but sadly they all died young, the two boys died before the age of one year, their daughter Lucy died when she was fifteen-years-old, a year after John was killed oversees. The pistol, along with a few other artifacts, was donated to the museum by Effie after John's death. Effie died in Saskatoon on May 19, 1951 at eighty-four-years-old. Imagine the stories she must have been able to tell!

Even though we have a close relationship with America, we are separated by a border. The American gun laws are considerably different than Canadian gun laws, and when the dynamics of the Department of Homeland Security and the Canadian Border Services Agency get involved, it becomes downright complicated to bring a gun from the USA to Canada.

The first problem was that the little pistol is now illegal in Canada; a firearm is not allowed to have a barrel shorter than 4.14 inches. The Iver Johnson pistol has a barrel of just three inches. Ironically, the law is such to discourage easy concealment, which is the reason why we think John Storer bought the pistol in the first place. It was a functional firearm too. The Americans test fired it, so it couldn't be brought in as an antique replica.

One thing you learn as a police officer is that there are regulations and laws for everything, often two or three for any situation. How the officer proceeds is usually made by weighing all the facts and using the right legal tool for the job. For example, someone is drunk and screaming on the street. If the responding officer feels the person will be okay if they are just removed from the area, they can be arrested for causing disturbance and moved away from the incident and released with or without charge. If the officer believes public interest is better served by the person sobering up before they are released, they can charge that person with municipal drunkenness in public and keep them locked up for a few hours.

In the circumstance that Tim Popp found himself in, he had to explore a number of ways to bring the pistol back. Although the pistol couldn't be imported, Tim realized that it was not actually being imported, it was being returned, as evidence to a crime. By rights, the theft from the museum was still an open file.

Everyone agreed that the pistol was in fact evidence to a crime. Once that hurdle was cleared, everything became easier. Chain of evidence is something that all police officers and border officers understand and the gun was shipped to the Havre Police Department in Montana. It was a matter of them driving the handgun to the US border crossing just south of the Canada customs station at Willow Creek.

Not everyone supported Tim's efforts in trying to get this little chunk of metal back home. The extra mile can be a lonely path and Tim found himself driving over six hours to the Willow Creek border crossing to pick up the "evidence" on his day off.

At the border all the services involved were happy to be seeing the gun safely home. With the traditional exchange of shoulder flashes (police patches) and some thankful handshakes, Tim was on his way home with the pistol.

The little gun still holds its secrets though. What happened to it between 1966 and 2009? Did it protect someone when they needed it? Was it used in a crime? Sandford police reported that it had been fired: fired at who or what? Perhaps there is a chapter or two left to know about this artifact that someday may be known.

With it all behind him, and the gun safely returned to its starting point at Fort Battleford, Tim still gets asked by colleagues, "Why bother?"

It's just a little gun. It's not very valuable; it's maybe worth about five-hundred dollars to a collector. It wasn't actually used in the North West Rebellion, so it's not a national artifact. John Storer wasn't a prime minster nor was he a great war hero. It's really just a conversation piece. So, why all the effort?

By Tim making the effort, by showing that the artifact has value, he was able to retell the story of Sergeant John Storer, a Mountie who lived a century ago, a First World War casualty who deserves to be remembered. By following the trail of the gun, Sergeant John Storer, if even for the briefest of seconds, was alive again in the hearts of the people who were on the investigative trail. They were able to take a few steps in his shoes and walk through pivotal times in the creation of Canada and the RCMP as we know it today.

The true essence of history can be easily forgotten. It can quickly become a list of dates and agreed upon facts easily read online or in a book. Tim and the others who helped bring this gun home got to participate, tell the stories, and play a part in the story. They got to experience what has come before and see how it is a part of what is now.

And maybe, just maybe, in a hundred years, someone will find some little trinket of ours and tell our story too.

Police Service Dog Memphis and Constable
Aaron Sheedy (Photo by Yolanda Romanec)

Constable Aaron Sheedy hails from Orillia, Ontario, and joined the RCMP
after a career in outdoor education. He was posted to the Toronto Airport
Detachment out of Depot, and has spent the last nine years investigating
drug importations and corruption at the Lester B. Pearson International
Airport. In addition to Aaron's daily policing duties, he is also a Narcot-
ics Detector-Dog Handler and a member of the Ontario Tactical Troop.
Aaron's policing duties have taken him from sea to sea in Canada, plus the
Arctic.

Aaron draws from his policing experiences, the people he meets, his trav-
els, and the natural world to write fiction and non-fiction with a predomi-
nately Canadian bent. Aaron lives and writes in Caledon, Ontario, Canada.